Cruising Wrinkles
Thomas Colvin

Also by Thomas Colvin
Cruising Designs
Cruising As A Way Of Life

Cruising Wrinkles
Thomas Colvin

Seven Seas Press, Inc.
Newport, Rhode Island

Published By:
Seven Seas Press, Inc.
Newport, Rhode Island 02840

Copyright © 1972 by Thomas Colvin

Second printing 1973
Third printing 1975
Fourth printing 1979
Fifth printing 1983

13579 TS/TS 08642

ISBN: 0-915160-14-5

Printed in the United States of America

Dedication

Life is full of beginnings because starting is easy, but what of finishes?
This book is for Jean who has always been not only an eager starter but,
more importantly, has remained to the end participating in the finish.

Contents

Foreword

It was inevitable, I suppose, that someday I would write a book, for I have written thousands of letters, numerous technical papers and semi-technical articles, always about sailing vessels, their construction, rigs and gear, the sea, cruising and navigation. I am a procrastinator; I am a sailor; I am a designer and builder of sailing vessels; I am dogmatic in my ideas until such time as I find something better—I am all of these things first; only lastly am I a writer.

I wish that I could relate a vivid moment in life when I felt compelled to stray into this rather awesome field, for I realize only too well that for many, the written word is the law, the Holy Grail, or what-have-you, and that when something is written, more credence must be attached to it than to a verbal account.

Bear with me in this book as I am not laying down the law. I am only trying to provoke some thought on the reader's part with some observations I've gathered over the years. If you agree with me in whole or in part, or if you disagree with me entirely, then this effort will have been worth it, for it means you have thought about these ideas.

I have ceased to be a crusader, but I am not yet content to be one of the silent majority. Like many others since the beginning of time, I heard the drum, I liked the tune, and I fell in with the march only to discover that I was not in step; so, I left the crowd to seek my own truths and ways. Without trying to be one, I find that I have become something of a non-conformist.

However, from all of this, one truth seems to stand out, and that is—because something is possibly possible, it doesn't follow that it is necessarily necessary. From this premise, I have designed, built and sailed vessels of my own design, never ceasing to learn and profit from my own mistakes and from observing those of others.

The list of those who have encouraged me over the years would be endless; however, with regard to writing, the late Ham deFontaine of *Yachting*, Mark Penzer of *Rudder*, and Moulton Farnham of *Boating* have been most inspiring and helpful. Steve Doherty, my friend and my publisher, has not only endorsed my writing ability, but has been doggedly persistent about getting me to put on paper my approach to some aspects of cruising which seem to be at variance with those of my contemporaries. Being a cruising man, Steve observed that some things I consider matter-of-fact might very well plug some gaps that are still open to others—in the consideration of a cruising vessel.

My wife, Jean, has put up with me for about 20 years now and has not only been a partner and shipmate, but has transcribed and typed all of my manuscripts and edited them. She has been a sounding board for the many tangents I have pursued, not to mention adapting to a sometimes hectic and unsettled way of life.

I would like to thank the editor of *Rudder*, Stuart James, for allowing me to reprint "Observations of a Non-Conformist," (1966), and "My Ideal Blue Water Cruiser," (1969). I would also like to express my thanks to Donna Doherty, who gave her professional touch to my informal sketches in this book.

Thomas E. Colvin
September 1971

Observations of a Non-Conformist

The ridicule directed toward any but the so-called contemporary rig is unjustified. Much of the contempt is based on fad and uninformed opinion. The relative merits of one rig versus another or of one sail cut opposed to another can be hypothetically expounded for hundreds of pages of meaningless garble including the full use of the Greek and Roman alphabets.

The dissertation would signify little.

It seems to me that the most logical method of finding the relative merits of rigs is to try several types on identical hulls. This is exactly what I did in a recent series of experiments; the test results were quite an eye opener.

There were a number of rigs which I could have tried, one against the other, but my finances and the size of the proposed vessel were both limited. Eliminated entirely were any of the square rigs or combinations thereof, because at best they are not suited to a man and wife crew. Furthermore, the displacement required to carry square sails would certainly be enormous compared to a fore-and-aft rigged vessel.

I eliminated the lateen not because it is inefficient but because of the tremendous amount of physical labor required to heave the yard over the masthead when tacking. I have done it and have seen it done many times, but the lateen rig does require carrying various sizes of sails and has no practical way of being reefed. In other words, this rig was for the medieval "yachtsman" with his bags and bags of sails to suit varying wind conditions.

For a number of years I have been interested in the Chinese lug rig. Having had experience in sailing this rig, I was impressed with its relative ease of handling. Like a lot of other prejudiced Occidentals however, I sort of scoffed at the appearance of the hull and the tattered, torn mat sails. However, I could never fail but be impressed by the lug's handiness under sail.

The question that kept recurring was: If the rig were introduced to a western hull rather than the eastern hull form, would the rig prove equal, better, or inferior to Western rigs?

With this in mind, I made a model of the rig, which sat around

13

for several years. In the meantime, Colonel Hasler sailed his *Jester*, a Chinese lug rig stepped on a Folkboat, in the first Single-Handed Trans-Atlantic Race. However, Colonel Hasler's rig was more of the northern type seen around Amoy where the junks have very narrow sails; whereas, I was more familiar with the southern rig that I had seen on the ocean junks. They have a low sail with a very full curve to the leech. I decided to use the Chinese rig on the sharpie hull since there were three other identical hulls of my design and construction in the same locality. Comparison of rigs, therefore, was predicated on having identical or near identical hulls available as trial horses, not because any one rig was suited only to one type of hull.

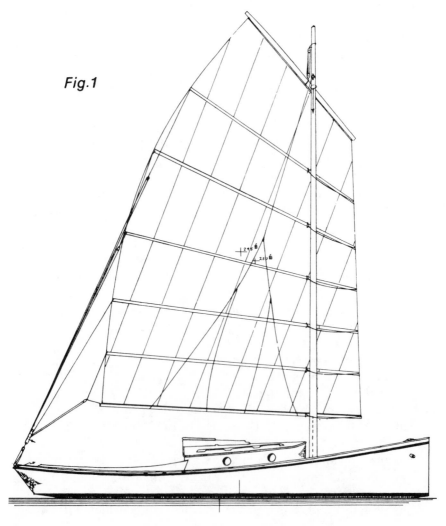

Fig.1

The sharpie has long been a favorite of mine, not only for cruising and sailing, but for use as an experimental hull in lieu of tank testing. Experimental sharpies have provided an inexpensive method of testing centerboards, leeboards, keels, rudder shapes, various methods of construction, as well as rigs and rigging. The data derived can be extrapolated or interpolated with relative ease. The full size sharpie permits the observer to be on the vessel being tested without having to predetermine leeway, apparent angles of the wind, or sea conditions. The observer doesn't have to introduce "fudge" factors to compensate for irregularities in the results as would be necessary in tank testing. Furthermore, direct alterations can be made and evaluated quickly.

Pandora, aptly named, was a 26' sharpie of steel construction. Her actual dimensions were 26'-4½" on deck, 7'-½" beam, 2600 pounds displacement without cruising gear, 3000 pounds with cruising gear, 800 pounds of ballast, no engine, four berths, a small water closet, galley, and self-bailing cockpit. She, like the others, was fitted with a fin keel with a total of 25" of draft, and an independently hung spade rudder.

The Chinese lug rig as finally built is shown in Figure One. Simplicity of the rig is at once apparent. There is one halyard, one snotter to hold the head spar to the mast, one sheet, one continuous leech line (sheetlets), lazy jacks, and no standing rigging of any type. Lazy jacks are normally set for furled position and are not adjusted when the sail is up. In a year of sailing, no chafe has been caused to the sail either by lazy jacks or by the mast. In fact, the rig, en toto, is very easy on all of its gear, more so than conventional Western rigs.

On all points of sailing, the lug rig seemed to be equal to conventional Western rigs. Exhaustive trials were carried out to make me fully familiar with the rig in varying conditions from calms to Force 8 winds. Contrary to popular belief, the flatness of the sail was not a detriment in light weather and the sail appeared to achieve the perfect shape in 10 to 15 knot winds. This is the ideal foil shape, however, and not necessarily the ideal for driving the hull.

The test results clearly stressed that the Chinese had really developed a remarkable rig. Its advantages include ease of setting, and complete control over the sail's leech, permitting adjustment of drive; i.e., the slacking off of the upper portion to spill wind in heavy weather. In fact, adjustments of the leech are so infinite they defy description. After some experience with the rig, one automatically senses the adjustments to achieve maximum sail drive.

Reefing involves merely slacking off the halyard and adjusting the snotter. It takes less than a minute. Another advantage of the rig: as soon as the halyard is eased and another batten drops to the lowest batten, the sail automatically slacks itself off, thus spilling even more of the wind. For the single-hander, this is a real asset. After dropping two or more battens, which can be done just as fast as one batten, the leech lines must be readjusted; but this is not mandatory until after the halyard and the snotter are secure. Then at one's leisure, the leech lines are shortened and the vessel is again capable of sailing from close-hauled to running or reaching.

Depending on the wind force and the heading, it is sometimes desirable to pass a tie around the lowered battens at their forward ends. This is especially true when you're close-hauled. Reefing or raising and lowering the sail can be done with the wind at any relative position to the hull. With the wind either aft or forward, the sail goes up and down with absolutely no trouble.

Because of the sail's shape there is little or no change in the center of effort as the battens are dropped forming the reefs. In fact, with adjustment of the snotter, it is possible to alter the sail's center of effort as much as 10% of the waterline. After the completion of trials, I was firmly convinced that it was the easiest and simplest rig I had ever sailed, and its adaptation to a western hull form was practical and feasible.

For the single-handed sailor or those just desiring a rig that requires very little effort on the part of the helmsman or crew, the Chinese lug rig seems ideal. As previously mentioned, the upper portion of the sail does not sag off unless it is intentionally slacked. Whereas a vang can be used on a conventional gaff, there is no intermediate control between gaff and boom; however, the Chinese rig allows control at *each* of the five battens.

Unlike Colonel Hasler's *Jester*, my *Pandora* is rigged true Chinese fashion—that is, the leech lines are completely independent of the sheet. All leech lines or sheetlets are led to a common wooden friction block. The sheet is then attached to the opposite end of this block. Thus, in theory and in practice, as the sheet is eased, the sail can move out with the same set. With the exception of the uppermost batten, which has a standard western block with a sheave, all others are friction blocks. In winds of over 10 knots, the sail automatically assumes even tension on each of the battens, and thus is in essence self-trimming.

I did not experiment with the method used on *Jester*, that is, with the sheet being common to all battens. Perhaps it is an improvement over the Chinese method. In my opinion, though, it does not permit the fineness of control that the Chinese method allows.

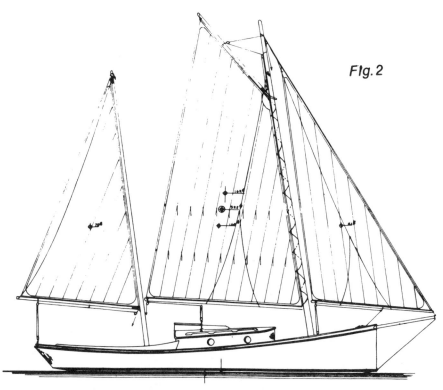

Fig. 2

In common with all rigs, as the luff is reduced, the ability to work to windward is reduced; however, the characteristic is not as marked in the Chinese lug as in the conventional western rig—say, the ketch, or for that matter, the gaff-rigged cat. The lug lends itself to total handling from the cockpit. Also, the simplicity of reefing allows one to carry sail much longer than would be dared with a western rig. All in all, it is the simplest and handiest rig that I have ever sailed, and in spite of its odd appearance by our standards, the experience of sailing such a rig is thoroughly enjoyable.

The rig has limitations.

For one thing, it cannot be hove-to. There is no such thing as letting her come into the wind and sitting there, for with the balanced lug, she is always off on one tack or the other. In very light weather, it is possible to get the vessel so the wind is abeam and ease the sheet so the sail is at right angles. Then the hull itself with its attendant leeway seems to create enough drag to effectively permit you to stay stationary. But in any sort of breeze, especially with a light displacement hull, she always wants to sail.

When not sailing in company with another vessel, it is quite easy to draw conclusions not necessarily valid. So, the author borrowed a jib-headed 26′ sharpie as a trial horse. This rig is shown in Figure

17

Three.

For a jib-headed rig, it is certainly a simple one. It is self-tending in coming about, has within four square feet the identical amount of sail area, and has very similar luff measurements to the Chinese lug rig.

I had some apprehension as the trials got under way. I knew from experience that the jib-headed ketch had proved a good all-around rig, could be tacked quickly and was especially able hard on the wind. To my eyes, the jib-headed ketch looked much trimmer than the great big lug sail, but after the first five minutes of sailing competitively against one another, it became apparent that any doubts I had as to the ability of the Chinese lug were groundless.

While the Chinese lug was certainly not faster when close-hauled, it was by no means slower. She pointed just as high, footed about the same, and she neither gained nor lost on the jib-headed ketch. After a four-mile beat to windward, the sheets were eased and the Chinese lug immediately pulled ahead of the ketch. Before the wind, she is a good 50% faster. Of course, a great deal of this can be attributed to having one large sail versus the three smaller ones. No doubt, a truer comparison could be made had the Chinese lug had two masts rather than one. The reason for one mast was that the hull form did not lend itself to the addition of a second mast without double sheeting the mizzen or putting on an extremely long boomkin. In a larger hull, it would have been feasible; and perhaps some of the objections, especially the windward ability in heavy weather, would have been obviated had two smaller sails been used instead of a single large one. This would certainly have increased the aggregate luff length to the advantage of the lug.

The trials were continued through a variety of wind condtions, and in every instance the results were practically identical. In extremely light weather, that is, calms to just the faintest of cat's paws, the Chinese lug with one large sail was infinitely more efficient than three smaller sails. But from three knots of wind up, the conditions always remained the same.

One interesting feature was that in Force 6 or Force 7 winds, the ketch was better hard on the wind than the Chinese lug. The crew's ability to manipulate mizzen and jib allowed her to work closer to the wind on the windward leg. But in another trial where we started off in light airs and the wind freshened to the point where reefing was mandatory, the Chinese lug, in being able to reef instantaneously in varying degrees as the wind freshened, was able to work out a considerable lead over the jib-headed ketch.

So, it would seem that, in a long range projection, the Chinese lug can be considered equal to or better than the jib-headed ketch.

The Chinese sail was vertically cut whereas the jib-headed ketch rig, of course, was cross-cut. The sails were made by the same sailmaker.

The next rig I investigated was the gaff ketch shown in Figure Two. This rig has considerably more area than either the lug or the jib-headed ketch, over 10% more. This, in some ways, detracts from the comparison drawn between it and the other two rigs. However, if the gaff rig is as inefficient as one is supposed to believe, then it should have made little difference in the final results. In most yacht club discussions the foregone conclusion seems that the gaff is a brute, a man-killer, a horrible rig on the wind, sags off badly, and has all the ills imaginable.

To prove their point, club foyer theoreticians select three or four old, amost derelict vessels with patched, rotting sails and hold these up as shining examples of the gaff rig's inefficiency.

So *Pandora* then became a gaff-rigged ketch.

If all that we read today can be believed, it should have been obvious that the jib-headed ketch would walk away from the gaff ketch when hard on the wind. Nothing could be farther from the truth. Since the gaff ketch had almost the same luff length as the jib headed ketch, identical jibs except that it was built without round, and the sails were vertically cut rather than cross-cut and without battens, over a four-mile course, she seemed to have a slight superiority. She was certainly no worse, and felt as though she were pointing and footing as well as the jib-headed ketch. But as soon as the sheets were started, away she went, leaving the jib-headed ketch behind. Off the wind there was no comparison. She was superior.

Compared to the Chinese lug, she about held her own through a broad reach, but on a run, even the gaff ketch showed its inferiority to the single Chinese lug. One would think that with the various theories abroad, the lacing of a sail to the mast would certainly destroy its efficiency. Perhaps it does, but from my observation, if it is less efficient, it is only minutely so.

In common, none of the rigs has shrouds. The gaff rig has only a headstay and the jib-headed rig has a head and a triatic stay. A further comparison between the two ketches is that they have the same number of sheets and halyards. The main halyard on the gaff rig is single, that is, the peak and the throat are one continuous halyard. The gaff ketch has a further advantage: It has lazy jacks for the mainsail which is certainly a blessing to anyone who does a great deal of single-handed sailing. Notice that the jibs on both the vessels are fitted with lazy jacks.

A comparison of handling ease of the three rigs might be expressed in the time required to get the vessel under way. This is from the time the dinghy is hooked to the mooring buoy and each skipper is on deck. It takes four minutes to get either the jib-headed or gaff-rigged ketch under way, only one minute and 30 seconds to get the Chinese lug under way. In coming back to the mooring and furling the rig, it takes just a little over five minutes to furl the jib headed ketch, four minutes for the gaff, and less than two for the Chinese lug. In other words, this is as one would leave the vessel moored for several weeks at a time, with everything tidied up. As far as lowering sails is concerned (and this is single-handed) the Chinese lug holds the record: 28 seconds from the time of round-ling up to the mooring, catching the mooring, securing it, then lowering the sails down in lazy jacks. The cost of rigging naturally favors the simplicity of the Chinese lug rig.

The jib-headed ketch is, of course, contemporary, blends well with any yachting fleet and certainly requires no mental strain on the part of the owner to accept. Without a doubt, it is extremely handy. Given a choice between the two, I much prefer the gaff to the jib headed rig. True, there are exceptions to the higher efficiency of the gaff rig versus the jib-headed, providing we are willing to add genoa jibs, spinnakers, mizzen staysails. However, in a small cruising vessel, at least, it should be mandatory that the space below be utilized for accommodations and not for sail stowage. We are only concerned with the efficiency of working rigs and not with the possible combinations of one, two, three or four times the working sail area in light sails.

If the racing rules would add together all of the sail area on board, not just the largest jib, but all sails with the exception of the storm trysail, including the area of the spinnakers, and add that into the formula, without a doubt, we would soon see some drastic changes in rigs and in hull forms. I believe that one of the reasons that the development of more efficient rigs has come almost to a standstill is that there is no real "cruising club," as such, in this country—in other words, like they have in Great Britain, where there is the Cruising Club and the Racing Club. Here, our Cruising Club is primarily concerned with racing, under the guise of cruising. I wish to state emphatically that I am in favor of racing, but I feel it should not be confused with cruising. I believe that if there were some recognition and promotion in this country for cruising yachts with rules encouraging the development of hulls, rigs, etc. without penalties, perhaps yachting would make a great stride forward within a few years.

During a recent boat show, I asked a number of prominent sail-makers their views on cross-cut versus vertical-cut sails. None really

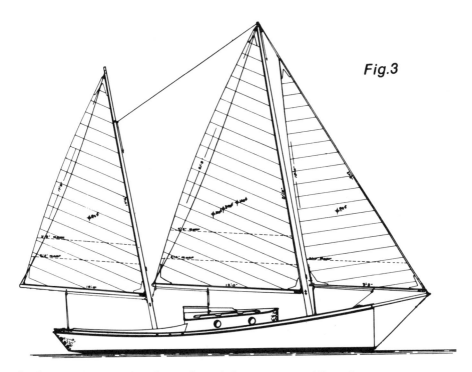

Fig.3

had an answer even when pinned down to specifics. Consensus was that the cross-cut must be more efficient because the majority of sails are cut that way now. Only a few of the cruising boats still have them cut up and down. When queried as to whether or not the increase in roach or round is the primary reason for cross-cutting (since it is free area under the new racing rules), they conceded that it was possible. I never did receive a definite answer as to the effect of the gores running up and down and the effect on the windward ability of the sail in percentile.

Now, if sail is 40% or 50% worse for vertical cutting, then vertical cutting should be abandoned by all. However, if it is only one to five percent worse, and then only close on the wind, it is worthwhile. It very happily eliminates the necessity of short battens and a flopping leech, both of which are a nuisance to any cruising vessel.

My conclusion is that the jib-headed rig is given more credit for efficiency than it deserves. The gaff rig is by no means obsolete and when properly designed can be as efficient as the jib-headed rig. The Chinese lug rig, as ancient as it is, can still give western rigs a run for their money.

On Cockpits

This supreme robber baron, vandal, thief, pirate, is found aboard too often, threatening the safety of a proper seagoing vessel: the cockpit. It has no place at sea. It is the weakest portion of the hull, structurally the most vulnerable, the one least capable of being freed after flooding. Indeed, in many boats today, it is more of a cocktail pit than a cockpit. It certainly is not a standing well, for there is rarely headroom under the boom that swings above it.

At present, most cockpits are equipped with inadequate scuppers, and are too large for the vessel. If the cockpit is flooded, the loss of the vessel is further threatened by the rise in center of gravity from these excessively large "containers." What purpose they achieve in a proper ocean cruiser I shall never know, for considering the additional bounty of uncluttered decks, they can be nothing but a menace. One has to stumble into and out of them, bark shins, etc., not to mention that they collect more dirt in port than any other portion of the hull. They require holes through the hull if they are to be freed below the waterline. In any case, there is no possible way of freeing a deep one even through the sides when the vessel is heeled; so this leaves the transom as the only drainage point. The cockpit's weakest link is the piping or hose and the cocks that connect them to the sea outside.

If one steers with a tiller and the vessel has any weather helm at all, he faces either port or starboard, and what a view of the world! For those fortunate enough to steer with a wheel, they have the advantage of being able to look forward, but all others in the crew can only see a side view of the earth, or they must become contortionists and twist and turn in the most awkward positions to see what is going on ahead.

Now a cockpit may be all right if we are thinking of racing rules where the height of the fore-triangle is based on the highest sheave from the deck; therefore, the boom is often very low in order to have adequate mainsail area based on this preconceived triangle. But why penalize an ocean cruiser with excessively low or short booms, low lifelines and pulpits, etc., when with a little forethought the height of the booms can be more than adequate for tacking—

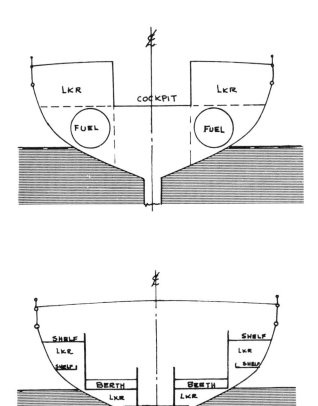

although inconvenient for powering—with a deck that can be walked from one end to the other without worrying about falling into a pit.

What about down below decks? Just think of the vast amount of room that can be utilized for a lazarette, an extra stateroom, accessibility to the engine should there be one, etc. All of these desirable possibilities are spoiled by a cockpit. In port, who wants to sit knee-to-knee when, with a nice uncluttered deck, deck chairs can be used —low-legged ones, of course? And who has to, or wants to, stay in the cockpit of a cruiser except for the poor bloke at the wheel? And who in a cruiser *needs* to stay in the cockpit if she is properly balanced?

All in all, a cockpit is merely a nuisance, a carry-over from not-too-thoughtful ancestors who were often trying to squeeze into something small what looked like something big to give them prestige. Of course, the present trend is even to compound the dangers of a cockpit even more by installing seat lockers that open up directly into the hull. The loss of a locker top in this case could cause flooding beyond the capabilities of most bilge-pumping systems.

In a 35' hull, the cockpit would cost approximately $500 to install and to pipe. If it is 3' x 5' x 18" deep, the loss is 22½ cubic feet of interior room. The pro-cockpit man says, "That's not much in a vessel of 900 cubic feet." *Wrong*—because without it, the gain is 150 cubic feet—a whole stateroom in some vessels! This is because the space outboard and abaft the cockpit is now accessible by a human, and even if he cannot stand up in this space at least he can be lying down. Believe me, there are many pleasures to be had by lying down!

Anchor Handling

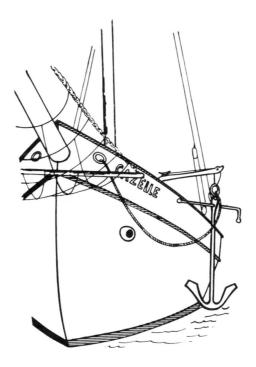

Some things can never be learned from a book despite what some authors would like you to believe. One of the many things that separates the men from the boys, the seamen from the lubbers, is their ability to cope with the various situations that are encountered in anchoring and in the handling of anchors. It is certainly sensible to peruse the many articles written on this subject, but practice and experience are the final teachers. It is ridiculous to think even for a moment that anyone could compile all the variations of anchoring situations (into tabular form) that you might meet in a lifetime of hooking your boat to the bottom for a meal and a good night's sleep.

Since most vessels today have auxiliary power, then the standard anchor windlass has convenience if nothing else. But all too often one sees a windlass aboard a vessel with 30-pound anchors. This is not a requirement. In fact, it is more of a nuisance. Until the weight of the working anchor reaches 50 pounds there is little necessity for having any paraphernalia to clutter up the foredeck. Above 50 pounds, it becomes desirable, and above 75 pounds almost mandatory unless there is one Samson in the crew.

There is more to anchoring than just dropping the anchor and getting it up again. The anchor has so many uses aboard a vessel that it is safe to say that the majority of vessels sailing today are improperly equipped to handle anchors. Furthermore, without an engine, the standard capstan (instead of a windlass) is probably one of the most useful items you can install. It is the only type of anchor-handling gear which permits a fair lead through 360°. Ideally, a capstan should be located almost amidships, but this is impossible on most yachts. However, even sited on the foredeck, it is surprising what can be accomplished with a proper capstan: Kedge off in any direction, lower a mast in a tabernacle (using sheer legs), heave down the vessel by halyard to get off a sandbar, etc.

In my years of cruising I have dragged every type anchor but one, and that is the yachtsman anchor, or kedge. All others I have had the dubious pleasure of dragging, up to six miles on one occasion, while I blissfully slept with a scope of 8-to-1. But not so with the kedge. On 3-to-1 scope, I sleep peacefully. On 5-to-1, I have ridden out gales, providing, of course, I used the proper size.

So the proper cruising vessel should make sure that her equipment is capable of handling anchors of suitable weight. My preference for raising them is to run a "whip" (single Spanish burton) from the masthead. This takes most of the work out of getting them aboard. But for dropping them, there is nothing like the old-fashioned catheads. This method is sure and clean.

Most people allow the chain or rode to come up directly from below decks. Perhaps as much as 99 times out of 100, this will suffice. But a sure-fire way of doing it properly is to range the chain or rode on the deck, the latter flaked to assure a run-out at least two times the depth of the proposed anchorage. Three times is even better. This is essential in a pure sailing vessel, as there must always be enough slack forward of the windlass for the anchor to hit the bottom before the chain comes tight. If the master fails to realize this, it is quite possible, especially in a seaway, to snap the chain, and he would find himself in a helpless situation of having neither room to tack nor sufficient way on to maneuver the vessel.

When a flying moor is necessary, one must run out the chain or rode for two anchors, but with the anchors set up on their catheads, very little effort is needed to drop them at the proper moment. And drop does not mean throw!

Deck Boxes

Well, we have eliminated the cockpit and the vulnerable lockers below it, and now we have to find a solution for the bits and pieces that are always lying on deck—mooring lines, chafing gear, sail stops, fenders, etc. In any good ocean cruiser, any item of equipment should serve more than one need, and so it is with deck boxes.

Properly constructed and fastened to the deck by bolting (that is, through-bolted on a wood hull or through-bolted to welded-on angle clips on a steel hull), we make boxes approximately 1/10th the length of the hull located to port and starboard on the cabin top, or deck if it's wide enough. They easily hold many more times the junk that is normally thrown in the cockpit seat lockers.

With a little forethought, we can incorporate a vent of the dorade type into this box. We will get more of an exhaust action from it than air intake, but the movement of air through the cabin in heavy weather certainly justifies their installation.

With still some more forethought, it is possible to mount the running lights either on the forward end or on the side of the deck box, the deck box then forming a suitable screen—added windage perhaps, but really convenient, and serving the dual—or triple—

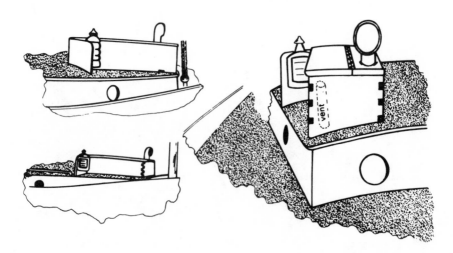

function mentioned above.

Furthermore, the area between these boxes can often be utilized as a site for the forehatch, giving it complete protection. The space between the boxes is a natural spot to stow other gear such as the outboard, extra warps, swimming ladder, or the storm anchor. Deck boxes make ideal seats, or a fine perch for sitting comfort when you are the lookout in foggy weather.

My Ideal Blue-Water Cruiser

My ideal blue-water cruising sailboat reflects, quite naturally, my personal taste in boats, the size and habits of my family, and my budget. She was to be, above all, comfortable, seaworthy, seakindly, fast and easily handled—requirements based on a series of intended voyages which includes non-stop passages, the shortest some 600 miles, the longest, 3500 miles. She was also to be suitable for daysailing, weekend sailing and general cruising in my home waters, Chesapeake Bay.

What sort of vessel meets all these requirements?

In my case, a lug-rigged steel schooner, 42′ on deck and 33′ on the waterline, with 11′-4½″ beam and 3′-10″ draft. Her displacement is 18,000 pounds of which 7500 is ballast. Her sail area is 854 sq. ft. on the wind and 1203 sq. ft. off the wind. Each of these factors is important, so let's investigate them in turn.

First, I am not speaking of a vessel on which my family of five would live with any permanence. I consider a 30- to 36-foot waterline length the smallest on which five could cruise with some comfort, and only when all five belong to the same family. But if the habits of the owner tend toward simplicity, as mine do, it is possible to have a fine, light-displacement blue-water cruiser on that waterline at a rather modest cost. My experience with light and ultra-light displacement has been quite favorable, so I had little hesitation in returning to the type for my new boat. Light displacement permits one to have a much larger vessel for a given displacement, resulting in longer waterline, more boat speed and more linear room in the interior. Surprisingly, for a given displacement the internal cube varies very little; a short fat, deep boat has about the same cubic as that of a long, lean, shoal vessel, but is not nearly as comfortable or as fast. My *Gazelle* is long, lean and light.

An engine, in spite of what many think, does influence the design of the hull, the concept of the rig, and one's general approach to cruising. One advantage of *not* having an engine aboard is never having to think about it. Careful planning can eliminate most of the noise and smell of an engine, but omitting it entirely reduces the cost of maintenance and eventual replacement, not to mention the

30

initial cost of the engine and installation. Propeller and aperture drag—which slows up the vessel more than one may realize—is also quite important. With no propeller dragging, any boat sails faster. During my 38 years of sailing, I have owned but one vessel with an auxiliary. It was used about 1/2 of 1% of the time—a dubious convenience for the expense involved. Most important,

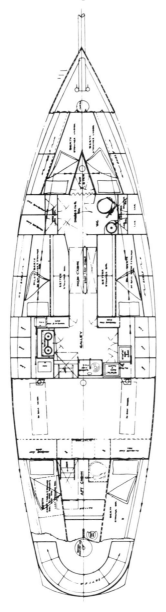

once an auxiliary is installed, even the best of sailors will subconsciously depend on it in an emergency and use it when sail and good, alert seamanship should suffice. Most of the boat accidents I have seen involving stranding or loss of vessel have been due to failure of the engine to start or to accomplish what good seamanship would have dictated be done under sail alone. Moreover, I maintain that there are few, if any, ports in the world that cannot be entered under sail, using only patience, wind, sea and tide.

By not having an engine on *Gazelle*, we have a wonderful cargo hold. By not having a cockpit, it is even larger. Stores can be placed in readily accessible compartments and bins instead of below the cabin sole. Access to the hold is from both cabins, so it also makes an excellent hanging locker for shore-going clothes, in addition to providing four lockers within the vessel.

My wife is neither physically strong nor large enough to do a man's work, and I do not expect her to—she just says I do. Taking care of three children, preparing meals and doing her trick at the wheel are more than her share of the work. So for all practical purposes, the vessel had to be a single-hander. And personally, I would not own a vessel I couldn't sail alone with ease.

There are few vessels that can match a schooner for efficiency, besides which it is so easily handled that one can tend lots of sail with a very small crew—namely me. Topsails and a powerful fisherman or main topmast staysail can be set for fine reaching performance, and multiple masts allow more combinations of heavy weather sail distribution with less effort, a definite plus in ocean cruising. Another plus is *Gazelle*'s Chinese lug rig, which I've found not only efficient and easy to handle, but surprisingly inexpensive both in initial cost and in maintenance.

For a light displacement vessel our *Gazelle* is not at all stingy with sail, and she does well on all points of sailing in all weather up to Force 8. Her sail area, divided by displacement to the 2/3 power, is 212. Her sail area to wetted surface ratio is 2.11 by the wind, 2.71 off the wind. Her narrow beam necessitates reefing for comfort by the time Force 5 is reached, easily done because numerous combinations are available as the lugsail's battens are lowered one by one. Because of its extreme flatness and control of all the battens from deck, the lug rig is good both on and off the wind. If we also assume that, for ocean cruising, the closest anyone would choose to sail would be five points or more to the wind, why stress the ability to point higher at the sacrifice of efficiency, ease of handling, and efficiency on other points of sailing?

The question of lee shores immediately arises. I have been

"caught" on lee shores many times, both by error and by intent. To work off one requires the ability to carry sail—lots of it—plus a vessel that sails well and won't sag off in tacking. Even so, under some conditions a vessel the size of *Gazelle* may not be able to weather the lee shore; anchoring or running her ashore may be the only solutions.

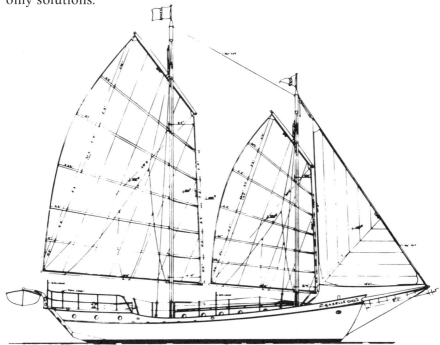

With regard to anchoring, modern anchor designs make it possible to use lighter anchor weights, but in practice the need for more chain and greater scope to insure sufficient holding power add up to about the same total weight as the old-fashioned yachtsman's or kedge anchor, which *Gazelle* carries, stowed on her foredeck. The advantage of the older anchors is that, while they may be more difficult to stow and to handle, it is possible to anchor in three times the depth of the water, opening many anchorages too cramped for use with lightweight anchors. With foredeck stowage it is possible to get a second anchor down in very tight anchorages. Provision can be made to prevent jib sheets from fouling deck-stowed anchors when under sail.

The same goes for *Gazelle*'s shoal draft—its advantages easily outweigh its drawbacks in reduced stability and less-than-breathtaking windward performance. The thousands of interesting places in this world with less than one fathom of water easily justifies shoal draft.

All blue-water sailing vessels are, in effect, cargo carriers. In order

33

to be self-sustaining, the vessel must carry, in addition to her crew and normal cruising gear, much larger quantities of food, water, linen, clothing, books, tools, charts, spare parts, and various other supplies. I usually figure eight pounds per person per day to be ample for cruising. This allows each person five pounds of water (maximum), and three pounds of food and other consumables.

As far as navigational equipment is concerned, I concede that many modern instruments are good and even convenient, but I do doubt their long-term reliability. For shoal water, I use a sounding pole; for deeper water, a sounding lead, armed if necessary. I also prefer a taffrail log as it can be streamed only when desired, then oiled and stowed in its box, where it should have almost unlimited life. Although I carry a radio direction finder, I also carry a chronometer. My celestial navigation is done via the old time-sight method most of the time.

I believe that it is a mistake to design a hull around an interior, but at the same time, I recognize that the necessities of rudimentary comfort must be provided. The idea of a double bunk is appealing, but I like to have an additional sea berth for heavy weather—one that is snug and can be slept in without undue tossing about.

We use both coal and primus kerosene stoves in the galley. My wife likes a double sink in the galley and a basin in the head. Speaking of heads, our two are the self-contained, hand-operated, chemical type (glorified cedar buckets), which comply with present regulations. As a result, there are no through-hull fittings below the waterline and only three above it—two sink outlets and a bilge pump discharge. Happily, my family does not need or desire an icebox or refrigerator, luxury gear which would only complicate an otherwise simple and convenient layout. For those who desire one, there is an excellent kerosene-operated refrigerator on the market which, with slight modification, can be made to work even on a rolling sailing vessel.

We also have no electricity—the RDF and binnacle light are battery-powered and our lights are candle lamps or kerosene lamps which have been faithful cruising companions for many years. Because of my belief in adequate ventilation, there are 22 opening portholes in *Gazelle*, one skylight, and three hatches, two of which are companionways.

For ease of maintenance and reliability, we use painted heavy-wall aluminum pipe for spars and bowsprit. We also use galvanized iron standing rigging for long-term reliability (no stress corrosion), greased or oiled three or four times a year. We use deadeyes and lanyards which do not freeze or corrode. All running rigging is dacron.

The hull of *Gazelle*, constructed of 10-gauge Cor-ten steel, for strength and light weight, had been sandblasted and metalized with molten aluminum prior to painting. Movement around the cabin trunk on deck is excellent because there is only one fitting, a pad eye, on the side decks. Cleats and belaying pins are either mounted on the rail aft, on the raised deck at the break, or on the side of the cabin trunk. For kedging off when grounded, I find a hand-operated capstan on the foredeck better than a windlass because it can lead fair through 360°. *Gazelle*'s two homemade halyard winches are very simply constructed and permit both main and foresail to be reefed without uncoiling and recoiling the halyards. The winch's axle is made from Volkswagen wheel spindles, encased in permanently grease-packed watertight housings, bolted to the forward and after ends of the cabin trunk.

What about performance of this dream design? The rig has turned out well beyond my greatest expectations. She balances on all

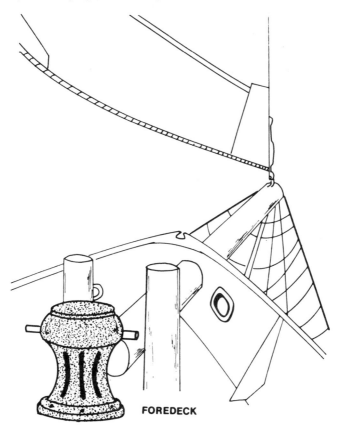

FOREDECK

points of sailing, requires no one at the wheel under most conditions, and only minor attention when running off in heavy weather. The schooner is at a disadvantage dead before the wind for, unless she is wing and wing, the mainsail blankets the foresail so the hull is really being driven by the mainsail alone. In light weather, this is of little consequence, but in stronger airs it can lead to a heavy helm. With lug rigs, the main blankets the foresail better than on a conventional schooner, so while it is possible to use preventers to go wing and wing up to Force 4 or 5, we increase our speed so much by sailing off a couple of points that it more than justifies not running dead before the wind. On all other points of sailing, regardless of weather conditions, *Gazelle* is self-steering or can be made to self-steer. She carries about two spokes of lee helm in light weather, neutral helm at about Force 3 or 4 and two spokes of weather helm in Force 5 and 6 winds.

As to hull form, there is little to be desired. She is very easily driven and very fast. Under foresail and jib, close-reaching, she's done 8 knots for several hours at a time. From calm to Force 4 winds, we sailed 48 nautical miles at 3.5 knots in absolute comfort. Reaching, under ideal conditions with Force 5 winds, we averaged 8.9 knots between buoys of 2.5 miles (though she was becoming heavy on the helm) and we even surfed her once though we don't know her exact speed that time. Throughout a variety of conditions, I can predict consistent 125-miles days with *Gazelle*.

As to stability, *Gazelle* likes 10° to 15° of heel. She hardens up at 18° to 20°, and it would take more wind that we have faced to bury her rail. She has proved that she can be driven hard to windward when other boats are using power for the same job. In spite of her shoal draft, she has more than enough lateral plane.

Gazelle was built in a year of my spare time; however, materials had been collected for almost three years before, and a number of items used in her are from other vessels I have owned.

Material cost breaks down as follows: steel, $2000; spar material, $500; interior joiner woods, linoleum, etc., $800; stoves, sinks, toilets, interior lamps, mattresses and cushions, $1000; four water tanks and piping, running lights, rigging, steering gear, compass and ventilators, $1500; sandblasting, metalizing, and interior and exterior painting, $1500; portlights, screens and hatches, $500; dinghy and davits, $650. Between 3000 and 4000 man hours of labor were involved in construction and outfitting. The sails are of 10 oz. Vivatex which cost less than $100 for material, including the dacron thread, plus $50 for bolt ropes and grommets and 100 hours of my time to loft and sew them. With labor at $5 to $6 an hour, it was possible to build my ideal blue-water sailboat, equipped and ready for sea, for under $30,000.

Fast, cheap and fully found, that's my *Gazelle*. There are no frills, a few conveniences and a few of my own weaknesses indulged. By "modern" standards the sailors we meet must think we're still sailing in the Middle Ages. But we're able to sail immediately and at any time from here to the other side of almost any ocean quickly and comfortably. To me, that's what a blue-water boat is all about.

On Binnacles

Today, too many compasses seen on serious vessels are in the "gadget" class, and are of dubious value to the master. Indeed, too often they are out of adjustment, compensated haphazardly—reliability nil. Although required if one is to steer a course at sea, through fog, at night, or when landmarks are unavailable for navigation, the compass seems to get a low ranking in the equipment budget. Nice shiny winches costing hundreds of dollars—and a $14 compass. This might not be too bad as some $14 compasses are sufficiently accurate to do a reasonable amount of navigation, but when the compass is mounted so that other gear gets priority locations, rather than in its actual proper place, (which means fixed and not movable or temporary) this is dereliction by the master. The compass should be given a most prominent place aboard the vessel.

The compass should be contained in a binnacle or a pseudo-binnacle that is *as robust as* any other protective feature of the hull. Indeed, it should be as strong and as well-mounted as the mast. It should be rigged so that nothing can hurt it. The compensating magnets should be well-secured and positioned in such a way that it is impossible to move them. The quadranal spheres, if used, should be surrounded by tubing or other structures that will prohibit fouling by sheets or somebody accidently grabbing them if the vessel lurches at sea.

So we come to the proper binnacle. It can be made of wood, aluminum, or, I guess, of reinforced plastics, providing in each case that it can be secured so that walking on deck does not transmit vibrations to it, and that it does not sag off when the vessel heels. If the binnacle is metal, it is best to flange the base so that at least eight bolts can fasten it through the deck. If made of wood, it should have at least four bolts plus a central bolt of monel running down from just under the upper platform to an eye bolt in the deck which is tensioned with a bronze turnbuckle. The outside should be encircled with a hoop of aluminum or stainless steel, preferably the former. It should sit at a convenient height to the person at the wheel. There is a craze today for a round pedestal. I think this is a poor choice, however, for, with a square top on it, one can take

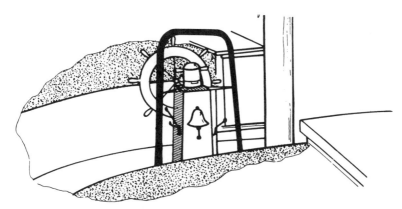

very quick relative bearings.

The binnacle should also be set up with a hood or cover for the compass for use in sunlight, and it should have adequate lighting for use at night. The beta-light that is incorporated in many fine compasses is excellent on dark nights but almost totally useless on a bright moonlit night. So, while the former will take care of general usage and can serve on any battery that is used, a separate, independently powered light should be added for those nights that are marginal—i.e., with bright moonlight. I have always felt that the compass light should be separated from the ship's lighting system by use of a self-contained battery. Spares should be kept on hand. These last many months and provide the safety factor that is an all-important part of the vessel.

On Cargo Holds

Yachtsmen, yacht designers, and the advertising media refuse to admit that, in reality, a yacht or small ocean cruiser is basically a cargo vessel. She carries cargo: X number of human beings plus Y amount of fuel, Z pounds of food and other stores—all this being required to enable her to make a passage from port A to port B, carrying the crew in reasonable comfort with adequate stores and water and the necessary spares to handle emergencies.

In an effort to squeeze tenement housing conditions into these small vessels, most modern designers have used up much former stowage space for more and more berths—the old Quart-of-Beer-in-a-Pint-Pot principle. To the skipper who has one, there is nothing so often blessed as a cargo hold, and the mate will appreciate the reduced boatkeeping chores resulting from the vast amount of junk that a cargo hold absorbs.

Located amidships, the cargo hold should extend across the whole breadth of the vessel and fill the depth. It may have a passageway through it, but it should be an area where one just puts stores, not a paying cargo. This, in turn, will enable the designers and the owners to have more livable quarters with fewer built-in lockers in numbers, though not in area. Ordinary ship's stores and food supplies could be stowed there as they would be normally, but the voyage stores could also be kept in deep bins or other lockers, built into the cargo hold. The addition or subtraction of this weight, located amidships, would not seriously affect the trim of the vessel. Shopping out of the cargo hold could be done once a week, transferring the necessary goods to the galley lockers.

If the cargo hold is not to be used for anything other than voyage stores, then the water tanks might be located here. The top of each tank would form a perfect bin. And even if the vessel were eventually to carry the proverbial "lost treasure" or just a mundane freight paying cargo, the water tank location would not interfere if proper dunnage were used. In a 35-foot vessel, a cargo hold about 3' long is possible; in 40', about 4'; in 50', about 5' to 6'.

It's hard to imagine what a really magnificient job of organizing the natural clutter of living afloat a cargo hold can provide, until you've lived with one for several years, as we have with ours aboard *Gazelle*.

Of Sail and Rig Chafe

Sins of Omission all too often lead to the loss of sailing vessels. There is no greater test of a seaman than his ability to observe, correct, and prevent chafe in the sails and rigging of a vessel. To many, a few clumps of baggy-wrinkle hanging aloft is enough to suggest saltiness of vessel and crew, but this is the only visible part—to an untrained eye. What about the hundreds of other unnoticed parts of the rig that are constantly being worn—such as sheaves, turnbuckles, shackle pins, halyards and sheets wearing on the nip, swivels, bolts and nuts—to name but a few? All these parts are subject to chafe.

Designers and builders often incorporate features that actually increase chafe, such as improper chain plates which require a toggle to correct a faulty shroud lead, undersized blocks, cleats sited too close to the masts, and sheet leads that go around corners or run against standing rigging. Blocks, of course, should be one size larger than the minimum even when using dacron for running rigging. The same rule applies to thimbles.

On a long voyage, the halyards should be adjusted daily to keep the nips fresh. Lazy jacks should float below their booms through fair leaders loose enough so the weather side can go taut and the lee slack. Turnbuckles should be of the "pipe" type with a Zerk grease fitting drilled and tapped in the center, and filled with grease. Shrouds, where the sail lays against them, should have baggy-wrinkle and so should topping lifts. Gaff jaws should be leathered as should the nock of a gaff sail. Parrells should be frequently checked against breakage.

The lifts and braces on a squaresail should be shortened as well as end-for-ended at frequent intervals. This also applies to halyards and sheets. Standing rigging should be slushed down at least every six months, and the seizings inspected for rust. Many items such as trade wind spinnakers, sheets and guys should be wormed, parcelled and served or at least leathered, for about a fathom where it rides the block. The gaff bridles and head stays are subject to great amounts of chafe, and should be checked as frequently as the jaws.

So a good sailor is constantly overhauling the vessel's gear. To quote an old bit of seagoing doggerel: "Six days thou shall work and do all you are able; And on the seventh, heave up and scrub the cable." The cable referred to the old hemp anchor rode that, after a prolonged stay in port, was encrusted with barnacles and worms. Is it any different today with nylon?

On Prisms

Our forefathers knew the value of light below decks and delivered it to the dark nooks and crannies where they needed it with a prism—a simple device of glass cut to multiple faces. In these days of electricity, prisms have almost passed out of use; at any rate, they are seen much more in England than in this country. Simpson-Lawrence, ship chandlers of Glasgow, Scotland, and Davey & Co., of London, England, both make a very robust prism with a galvanized iron frame.

Prisms serve their purpose so well that it seems a shame not to install them on most vessels. The best locations for them are in areas where installing electric lights poses a special problem; where sunlight does not reach; or when the vessel has a limited electric supply and the fewest lights possible are the best arrangement. Certainly, they are a boon in any dark corner of the hull where one must work or find stowed gear. Areas that come to mind are the chain locker, the cargo hold, the foc'sle, and the engine room. On vessels with an after peak or lazarette, prisms would also be very welcome. Three prisms in a large engine room, say in a large ocean-cruising auxiliary, would equal many, many light bulbs, and at no cost in battery drain.

Prisms are inexpensive to install and have an unlimited life expectancy, provided one does not drop a heavy hammer or marlin spike through them. Careful bedding of the frame will insure that there are no leaks at the edges of the cut-out hole. Of course, as we all know, no matter from where one might drop a spike, it is bound to land either on the skylight, on a prism, or on someone's foot!

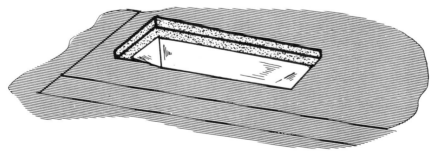

Sailing The Chinese Junk

Perhaps in a former life I was Chinese and, if not a sailor, I was at least a passenger on a junk. My mind seems instantly to reason out the many intricacies of the rigging and technique of sailing the Chinese lug rig, and the centuries of development of a Chinese lug rig appear to me quite logical. Perhaps this, in part, accounts for my attraction to the rig—because it *is* so logical. Almost nothing is incorporated just for appearance, although local tradition strongly determines various regional variations of the rig. With the omission of any one part, the rig will not function.

Some might think that once the basics are understood the mystery is solved. This is not so for there are hundreds of variations and combinations. To be able competently to sail the Chinese lug rig, one must first understand the principles underlying the concept of the rig, and the reason behind all the many parts that comprise the total rig. Also, one must not become dismayed by different types of rigging and blocks performing the same function. As stated above, there is a good, functional reason for each variation.

Battens

The most distinguishing feature of the Chinese lug sail is the full-length battens, which number anywhere from four to thirty. Battens help to keep the sail flat, allowing a junk-rigged vessel to sail closer to the wind. Most of the southern Chinese junks, many of which are sea-going types, have from five to ten battens per sail. Indeed, the number of battens per sail often varies depending on whether it is a fore, main or mizzen, and what waters are to be sailed. The inland junks of the Yangtze and Yellow Rivers have a larger number of battens per sail the farther upstream the vessel operates. The number of battens in a given sail generally determines its capability to windward. So a junk with many battens may be assumed to place a high priority on the ability to sail upwind and also to operate behind high banks of the various rivers. Some of the ocean-going junks of the northern provinces have many more battens than those of the southern junks because most of these vessels must operate in estuaries along the coast as well as on the high seas.

The Yard

Since I am interested more in the rig for ocean cruising and coastwise sailing, I have used the 5-, 6-, 8-, and 10-batten lug sails on vessels of my design. The Chinese balance lug sail always has a vertical luff, and from 1/6 to 1/3 of the sail is forward of the mast. It is hoisted on a yard (the upper spar) from a point from 1/3 to 1/2 of its length aft of the forward end. The sail is stiffened at predetermined intervals with lathes of bamboo or wood. The boom is actually the lowermost batten but of larger dimensions than the other battens, primarily to hold the weight of the sail when it drops into the lazy jacks. The boom does not function like a Western boom, so it does not require nearly as much strength. The yard in all Chinese sails is much heavier than the boom. Whether the sail is carried on the port or starboard side of the mast varies throughout China. In many places the sails are carried alternating port and starboard on different masts.

Euphroe

Near or at the aft end of each batten is attached a continuous line forming a spiderlike web, the parts of which are called "sheetlets." These sheetlets are rove through a block called a "euphroe." Very often, a sheetlet will be attached to *two* battens by a bridle. In this case, a dumbbell block (which can be either a friction block or a block with sheaves) is fitted to the bridle so that the sheetlet may be a continuous line. This reveals that sail flatness depends *not only* on the battens but *also* on the sheetlets. The methods of reaving the sheetlets are many, each one depending on how the sail will be used. In the ocean-going junks, the common way is to attach the standing part of the sheetlet to the upper battens. This permits the sheetlet to be shortened when reefing so as not to alter the relationship of the euphroe to the full sail when sailing closehauled. In the five-batten lug sail that I usually employ, the primary pull of the mainsheet or foresheet *is exerted on the whole sail.* On the other hand, the primary pull of the euphroe is always exerted at *the top* of the sail. In cargo-carrying junks where there are more than five battens per sail, the euphroes are fitted with a sheave, and there are at least *two* euphroes per sail. The sheet very definitely affects either the top half or the lower half of the sail. Because of bulky deck cargoes, the primary euphroe of the mainsail is always the lowermost one. This is arranged so that the sail can be reefed high in order to permit a deck load to be carried under it.

The foresail's primary euphroe *is* the top one. This seems to achieve the best control for close-hauled sailing as foremasts usually rake forward. Also, the sail seems to stand better when running off in heavy weather. On the mizzen, which is chiefly a steering sail, the primary euphroe is *always* the bottom one, since this sail is seldom reefed.

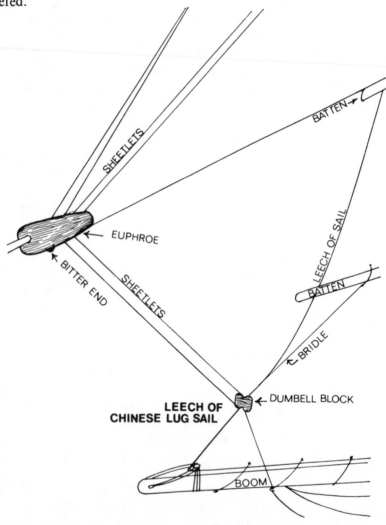

By manipulating the endless sheetlets, an infinite number of variations of shape and attitude can be put into the sail. For example, hauling the upper batten towards the centerline of the vessel would automatically release the lower batten and boom, permitting them to move farther outboard. Or, if the center batten is hauled inboard, it will simultaneously release the top and bottom half of the sail to increase their angle to the centerline of the vessel. The latter is a trick maneuver, however, and other than for demonstration purposes is really never used, but merely shows one of the many variations.

Normally, tension is introduced into the sail to achieve the best possible draft of the sail. For example, in closehauled work, once the sheetlets are set there is nothing further to do from tack to tack. When running, it is advantageous to slide the euphroe up so that it bears higher on the sail, thus giving more flatness to the lowermost battens and altering the shape of the sail for best downwind performance. In gybing, however, the relationship between the euphroe and the battens remains the same and no adjustment is necessary.

The battens greatly simplify reefing so that a sail can be carried longer in heavy weather, and the proportion of sail carried on the vessel will probably be greater than on a sister vessel rigged Western fashion. Chinese sails can be dropped very rapidly. And, since sheeting is to *each* batten, sails can be made of a much lighter sail cloth (or even an inferior grade of cloth) because the strain on the sail is so evenly distributed—unlike Western sails. Battens also perform the function of ratlines and allow one to climb aloft on them. In fact, photographs reveal that most Chinese junks have ratlines only in the upper 1/5 of their mast and always on the opposite side of the mast to which the sail is set, since the battens serve as ratlines on the lower part of the mast.

Parrells

Each batten has its own parrel around the mast. In some of the larger rigs a second, hauling parrel is used to adjust the fore and aft position of the sails and the weight at each batten. The sail is laced to the yard and laced to the boom or to a special, second bolt rope. In the case of a heavily raked foremast on the three-masted junks, it is necessary to have a "tack tackle" which not only bowses the sail aft to relieve the strain, but also alters the center of effort of this particular sail, fore and aft. This tackle also permits the sail to be used as a squaresail when running before the wind, and heaves it inboard when in port to keep it from projecting over the bow.

Lazy Jacks

All Chinese sails have topping lifts or lazy jacks, and the larger the sail, the more intricate these become. A Chinese sail is very heavy compared to its Western counterpart. The mainsail, boom and gaff on a 100′ gaff-rigged Western schooner, for example, will weigh somewhere between 1 and 1½ tons! On a 100′ Chinese junk, the mainsail, battens, boom and yard may weigh close to 3½ tons!! On *Gazelle*, the mainsail, battens, boom and yard weigh close to 500 pounds.

Chinese Sails

As noted earlier, the quality of cloth and the workmanship contained in a Chinese sail appears to be rather immaterial. For centuries, the Chinese used mat sails; today, cheap cotton is used. Regardless of the material, a Chinese sail is not only strong (because of the sheetlets and battens) but is also economical to construct. In a small Western type sail we often find as many as 180 stitches to the yard; however, the Chinese often use as few as 72 stitches to the yard—real homeward bounders!

Chinese sailcloth comes 11″ wide. European sailcloth is 24″ wide and American sailcloth 28″ wide; however, today, the synthetic and canvas cloths are usually either 32″ or 36″ wide. It is not necessary to "false seam" a Chinese sail. In way of the battens, the sails are reinforced with a chafing strip. The Chinese color their sails by

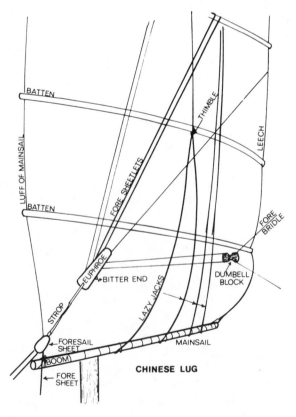

CHINESE LUG

dipping them in pre-boiled mangrove bark solution. The cheap cloth used in China seldom lasts more than two years without becoming ragged, at which time they are patched with any material available. Such a battened sail may be torn, or even full of holes, but with the support of the battens on the remaining cloth, they still draw well and function almost as well as when new. Of course, one advantage in having part of the sails blown out is that it saves reefing! We have sailed with a rather large hole in *Gazelle*'s foresail for over 1000 miles without having it tear any further, and without noticeable effect on the efficiency of the sail.

Masts

The mast in a Chinese rig must be *much stronger* than a Western mast since the sail is so heavy, and wind strength plus sail weight exert tremendous forces. It is better to design mast strength against bending rather than compression, so it is inadvisable to use turnbuckles in lieu of deadeyes when setting up the shrouds, if shrouds are to be carried at all. Actually, the majority of riverine junks do not carry *any* standing rigging. However, they *do* lead halyards, topping lifts, etc. to the side of the hull which helps reduce the whipping of the spar somewhat. In most of the vessels of my design, the standing rigging merely serves to dampen the whip of the mast in a seaway.

Sail Behavior

The Chinese sail does not luff; however, it does stall, so one of the first things to "unlearn" is watching the leading edge of the sail for a point of luff—it just does not exist. In fact, in the three-masted junks, it is possible to trim the sails to amidships and stop the vessel completely. The Chinese sail is always trying to sail, and the first thing one must learn to keep the hull moving by unlearning what he already knows about sail angle in the Western rig, and by studying the new hull-sail-wind angle relationship for this rig. There is no aid such as luffing to indicate when the sail angle is too close to the wind, so it becomes a matter of practice and judgment as to how to position the sails best for any given point of sailing. Needless to say, Chinese sails cannot be strapped-in tight amidships. When double sheeting is used, the position of the pad eye for the sheet is usually located so that when the boom is directly over it, the sail should not be sheeted any closer inboard for windward sailing. Most often, these pad eyes are located on the gallows frame.

The Snotter

Other parts of the rig include an adjustable yard parrel which I call a "snotter." In the total "up" position, it functions primarily to hold the yard against the mast, but when the sail is in various reefed positions, the snotter performs the additional function of holding the yard against the mast and allowing the sail to be peaked higher (by use of the topping lifts or lazy jacks). In the low, broad sail seen in South China, it is possible to alter the center of effort of the sail plan in the reefed condition (by approximately 10%) by topping-up the reefed portion of the sail and hauling the snotter, bringing the yard up snug against the mast. On the smaller Chinese sails, a downhaul is needed on the boom. Since there is seldom enough weight to this batten (or boom) so that it will hang down completely docile and hold all the cloths taut, it is rarely necessary to adjust the downhaul—except in the rare instance of reefing from the bottom upwards rather than from the top downwards.

Reefing

To reef a Chinese sail, one slacks away on the halyard until one, two, three or more battens fall, allowing them to come to rest on top of the boom, as the lazy jacks gather up the bunt of the sail. In the five-batten sail, when more than one batten is dropped, an adjustment must be made on the euphroe (as stated previously), and not until several reefs are added is an adjustment necessary. However, in the five-batten rig with the bridle, the bridle must be tied off—a simple overhand knot on the dumbbell block (this block is explained in the paragraph on "Euphroe.")

At the euphroe, the sheetlet is then shortened at the bitter end by a proportionate amount which then reorients the sail to its identical position before reefing. The wonderful discovery one makes as he reefs a Chinese sail is that, as soon as the reef is dropped (which takes about 30 seconds), the sail automatically pays out, thus relieving itself. In very heavy weather, I have always found it wise to take the extra length of the downhaul and pass it through the parrell, then back to the downhaul cleat to allow the sail to be set taut again; however, it is not essential that this be done immediately. As more reefs are put in, further adjustments are made to the length of sheetlet at the euphroe unless one is running off, when it is unnecessary to make any adjustments at the euphroe until after the third reef is taken. Since battens are not lashed down, additional or fewer reefs take only moments to accomplish. The Chinese sail, without a doubt, is the fastest reefing sail in the world. Also, the Chinese sail never fails to come down—in a flat calm or a blowing gale.

Lowering Sail

Lowering the sails on a Chinese lug rig is another great pleasure as there is *absolutely nothing further* to do upon releasing the halyard. The weight of the sail alone brings it and the battens down, even when running, and the folds are all gathered up by the lazy jacks. There are no ties to put on, nothing to lash down, nothing to gather by hand—just uncleat the halyard and walk away.

Having sailed Chinese junk-rigged vessels now for over seven years, I have discovered many advantages to the rig, plus a big reduction of work. In fact, as I write, it is inconceivable to me that I would ever return to any of the many Western rigs with which I have been shipmates. Sailing with the Chinese rig has made me very lazy, and further, weather conditions concern me far less than ever in light weather.

Reefing Gazelle

The procedure in preparing *Gazelle* for heavy weather is first, to stow the jib, and second, to double-reef the mainsail. Under this combination, she points as close as she did with the jib up and handles very much like a sloop. She is self-tending when tacking. At sea, when close or broad reaching, quite the opposite is done. The mainsail is either double or triple reefed as the wind increases and, when this is *still* too much sail area, this sail is handed and we continue with just foresail and jib. If the wind should increase to, say Force 7, we carry on with *just* the foresail.

The Chinese sail, since it is not subject to flogging, is a much kinder sail to carry in heavy weather, especially if one wants the vessel to round up, or if the vessel is beginning to yaw. It has been observed that the foresail is really a "Beaufort sail." That is, with only the foresail raised, the speed of the hull equals approximately the number of knots as the force of the wind . . . five knots in Force 5, seven knots in Force 7, etc. This was first ascertained by Dick Johnson in *Migrant* (a sister ship to *Gazelle*) on her passages from Nova Scotia to the Marquesas.

The foresail is seldom if ever reefed, but it *can* be reefed to slow down the vessel either in light weather or in heavy weather. As the force of the wind increases, and if continued downwind performance is still desired, then the jib is reset and sheeted flat amidships, the foresail is taken in altogether, and the vessel is held dead before the wind. The jib feathers from one side to the other, exposing very little area; yet, being well forward, this action discourages the vessel from yawing, and she keeps moving.

The Jib and Staysail

In passing, I might mention that one of the reasons why I added a jib to *Gazelle* was the uncertainty in my mind whether the rig would really function without it. Now, four years later, I must say that of all the sails, the jib is the most trouble to handle. In addition to the jib, I carry a triangular sail between the mastheads which might loosely be termed a fisherman, as it functions about halfway between that sail and the topmast staysail of a square-rigger. It has the advantage over a regular quadrilateral fisherman of not having to be dipped when coming about. This "fisherman" is set and sheeted like a flying jib.

Besides this, I also have a main staysail. This sail sets from the mainmast head to the deck forward of the foremast and is the same shape as a ketch's mizzen staysail. It is set flying and is seldom used except on long passages, as it does require being dipped and reset each time the vessel is tacked.

Gybing

Gybing in a Chinese lug rig is rather an amazing maneuver, primarily because of the utter lack of catastrophes. Indeed, the boom and the sail swing across the deck as fast as those of a Western rig; however, that last moment when it would normally be, "Goodbye, gooseneck," or perhaps even, "Goodbye mast!" nothing happens— just a little tug when the balance of the sail catches the wind and takes most of the weight out of the gybe.

Sailing The Chinese Rig

A single-masted Chinese lug rig is sailed in the same manner as a catboat. A two-masted Chinese lug rig is sailed very much like a cat ketch or a cat schooner. When fitted like *Gazelle* with a jib, a vessel is normally sailed and trimmed as a conventional schooner. A three-masted Chinese junk rig, on the other hand, is sailed more like a ketch, the foresail acting like a jib but with far greater control than a jib offers.

Three-Masted Junks

It is my opinion that the three-masted Chinese junk rig is the most convenient and handiest rig in the world. As on a ketch, the mizzen serves primarily as a steering sail. The mainsail, as on a ketch, is located amidships and is the largest sail, so the driving force is exerted on the forward part of the vessel rather than on the after part, as in the schooner. However, the foresail is the most versatile of the three sails for, with its "tack tackle," it is possible to bowse it well out to one side when running and get a full rap of wind even with the main set. Remember, the Chinese sail is really a balanced lug; therefore, when running, a substantial portion of the mainsail protrudes past the mast, opposite the main portion of the sail, which further aggravates the blanketing of the foresail. Because of this, by bowsing out the foresail, one exposes more sail area to the wind. In heavy weather, with the battens under full control on one side, the tack tackle of the foresail can be led aft to the bulwarks and used as a preventer, and then one virtually has a squaresail.

I have yet to figure out all the possible combinations of reefs in a Chinese sail, but I am sure there are *more* combinations than would ever be needed. With the straight luff of a Chinese lug sail, clear of any aerodynamic disturbances from the mast, it is a very weatherly rig and it is quite immaterial whether the masts stand straight or not. When this rig is coupled with a Chinese hull, one automatically benefits from the high poop in that, with no sails up, the vessel lies much closer to the wind than any of the Western hulls. In fact, it is odd that vessels built and rigged east of Suez, with no sail set, will lie ahull rather close to the wind; but, vessels from west of the Suez have a tendency to lie stern to the wind.

Chinese Sea Anchors

The Chinese are past masters in the use of a sea anchor. Usually they use a large conical basket rather than our type of conical canvas bag. I have made some rather interesting experiments using both the woven basket and a canvas bag of the same dimensions as a sea anchor. I have found that the woven basket has much greater efficiency in holding the vessel's head up to the seas because the numerous holes increase the drag. While the water that filters through the basket mesh (as the boat surges) imposes greater load on the various parts and lines, it is not subject to the whipping and jerking that the canvas bag must absorb.

An interesting experiment would be to take a conical sieve that is used in many kitchens for pureeing and find another conical shape of the same diameter such as a large fuel funnel, and then pull them both through the water. It will be found that the sieve creates more turbulence and drag.

Conclusion

It requires much practice to get maximum sailing performance out of a Chinese sail; however, once the rudiments are acquired, the finer points suggest themselves automatically, and it is not long before the "loada"—as the Chinese junkmaster is called—is able instinctively to set the sails to achieve the greatest efficiency for the desired course. At this point, sailing along on a fresh breeze, with the sun sparkling on the water, one may be justified in feeling just a bit smug about the cheap, handy, easily repaired and rugged rig overhead.

On Sailmaking

Modern propaganda would have us believe that to do their job properly, sails must be designed by a computer, run by very brainy youngsters who know how to manipulate them. Perhaps this is so. But it would be foolish to assume that our forefathers who made sails without computers were dunces. In fact, the weave of cloth with which they had to work in most cases was far inferior to anything that we have today. How bad must a suit of sails be not to work at all? I have never seen such a suit, and I have seen sails on all types of vessels all over the world. Indeed I cannot conceive of a sail so poorly made that it will not function. I don't mean to win races, but just propel the boat—and this is the function of sails.

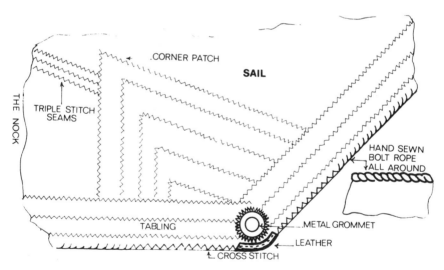

So, why shouldn't the owner have the pleasure of making a sail? If it blows out at sea, what is the catastrophe? He has made them; he knows how to remake them, make a new suit, or alter them. Today, the temptation is to hit the panic button the instant a sail tears. Of course, for the fortunate few there is always a replacement below decks they can bend on, after which they dash back to the sailmaker demanding why it happened and whether it can be prevented next time. I believe that it is necessary for the ocean-cruising man to spend a great deal of time learning all of the arts of the seaman, and this includes sailmaking.

There is no great secret to it. It is tedious work at times, and it can be frustrating, but it is better than beating your wife. The Great Debate over cotton versus dacron has been done to death. In the past, I used cotton when only cotton was available. Today, with new synthetics available, I still use cotton. In the tropics cotton will last as long as dacron since dacron cloth *is* attacked by tropical sunlight. I believe that colored dacron improves longevity in a sail. But dacron does have a greater problem—chafe—and it is more difficult to sew. It is an easier material to cut because the stretch allowances are not necessary, or are so small that in a cruising boat they need not be considered.

But with the computer as Sail Designer came the notion that the sail should not be touched with human hands, and so the considerable handwork that is proper for an ocean cruiser—hand-sewn eyes and hand-sewn bolt ropes all around, which make the sails stronger than the machine-sewn bolt ropes or taped sails—all these have almost gone by the board.

An excellent book on the subject of sailmaking is "Make Your Own Sails," by R. M. Bowker and S. A. Budd, is published by St. Martin's Press, Inc., New York, 1966. It gives the fundamentals, and with a little common sense the rest can be figured out. The small investment in this book could save one thousand times its cost in, say, a 45′ ocean cruiser. To be sure, the book does not cover everything, but there is one thing to remember—after making your own sails, if there is something you don't like about it, at least you know what not to do the next time.

On Steering Gears

There are all sorts of devices for steering; however, there are only a few reliable ones. Without a doubt, the simplest and most straight-forward is a tiller. The next adaptation is a tiller with lines leading to a drum. Today, the sophisticated, "modern" way of doing it is to have a quadrant, usually mounted in an inaccessible space below decks, leading with wires to a geared drum over which a chain is draped. According to the number of failures that occur, it evidently has the same drawbacks (at probably ten times the cost!) as the old sailing ship method of using just manila rope leading through a series of blocks on deck to the wheel.

The next method is via push-pull cables, which are subject to failure. Considering the number of decades they have been in use, the improvements in them seem minimal.

Another type of steering gear is the tooth quadrant, and this is very satisfactory, giving very little trouble, but it does require a considerable amount of space, and unless stops are fitted to the quadrant it will spin off.

Probably the most foolproof of them all is the worm steerer. I have seen this type steering gear on vessels over 60 years old, and have yet to see one fail, providing, of course, that they got a reason-able amount of maintenance—a bit of grease on the worm once in awhile. I have seen worm gear steerers with so much "slop" in them that I wondered how they could work with any reliability, yet they went on and on. So, for my money—and for reliability at sea— the best is the worm gear, excepting the tiller. On a vessel of any real size, the work required of the helmsman handling a tiller when a sea is running is so heavy that the worm gear type seems worth its weight in titanium winches—and this is even truer if the distaff members of the crew stand watches.

It's important to note that the worm-gear steerer stays where you leave her. That is, when you take your hand off a wheel spoke, the wheel does not move. While this characteristic means there is no feed-back from the rudder to the wheel, which some helmsmen like to feel, it also means that you can leave the helm unattended for short—or on some points of sailing, long—periods of time, to trim sails, duck below for a cup of coffee, or do jobs on the deck. On balance, this type steerer seems to offer much more than it loses on the cruising vessel.

I am one of the fortunate few who find tranquility, peace of mind, and happiness at sea. The vessel I am on is my world and it reaches to the horizon. Normally, my vessel has always been a self-steerer; therefore, when in a dinghy or swimming alongside, I have a sense of loneliness as I realize that it is quite possible for the boat to sail herself away. Even with someone on deck, I can never overcome this fear. It matters not what type of steering gear is used or if the wheel is put hard over, as a puff of wind will start her moving to the lee. Oh, those foolish souls who lash the helm and go for a swim while the others are below! Even moving at one knot, a strong swimmer would be hard put to catch up with the vessel—and who would know? So, as always, maximum caution is required at sea.

On Engines and Horsepower

It is surprising to discover how little horsepower is really required to propel a vessel at a hull speed—which is the square root of her waterline expressed in knots. It is even more surprising how little horsepower is ever needed or used at sea.

For an ocean cruising vessel, 1/2 horsepower per ton can be considered maximum. For coastwise cruising, one horsepower per ton is more than adequate. From the accompanying table, it is easy to see that the two factors that control speed for a given horsepower are waterline length and tonnage (2240 = 1 ton).

In selecting an engine, remember that diesels usually burn .45 pounds per horsepower hour. The larger the engine, the greater the fuel consumption which requires larger tanks, hence larger displacement, and so on *ad infinitum*. How much fuel should we carry? I recommend enough for 40 hours of smooth-water powering as maximum for all vessels; and for ocean cruising, 20 hours seems to be compatible with other factors that enter your considerations, such as the weight of other vital items that must be carried—stores, water, etc. An ideal engine should be slow speed, high torque with a large slow-turning propeller—running at a maximum of about 1000 RPM. Hand-start is the most reliable type and has the least that can go wrong with it.

What about propeller drag? Well, if this is a serious consideration, don't install an engine. I did without one for years and installed an engine only when I decided I needed the convenience of

TYPICAL HORSEPOWER REQUIREMENTS FOR A GIVEN WATERLINE LENGTH AT VARIOUS DISPLACEMENTS

WATER-LINE	TONS	SPEED IN KNOTS AT 10 HP	15 HP	20 HP	MAXIMUM USABLE HORSEPOWER	MAXIMUM SPEED
30 FT ...	5 ...	6.70 ..	7.30 ..	--	16.2	7.3
	10	5.60	6.15	6.60	35	7.3
	15	5.00	5.50	5.90	58	7.3
35 FT ...	10 ...	6.05 ..	6.70 ..	7.10	35	7.9
	15	5.35	5.90	6.40	58	7.9
	20 .	5.00	5.45	5.85	81	7.9
40 FT ...	15 ...	5.75 ..	6.35 ..	6.80	58	8.45
	20	5.35	5.85	6.25	81	8.45
	25	5.05	5.55	5.85	105	8.45

one. Whether it will prove that valuable is still open to debate.

A small, high-speed inefficient propeller is worse than no engine at all, and can get you into trouble when you really need push. So, if you want the most push and reliability for the least cost and trouble, then choose an engine with a few big-horses—not one with lots of little ponies.

Rebuilding Gazelle

A rising tide of discontent seemed to surround me each time I cruised aboard *Gazelle*. The vague center of this discontent always eluded my efforts to answer the question: What's wrong? So I posed the question: Why, if *Gazelle* fulfills my requirements for a blue-water cruiser, do I become so frustrated with her at times? Not until I had sailed her more than two and a half years and 3000 miles was I able to find an answer—and it was nothing spectacular in the end.

Gazelle was at her home moorings, and I had just finished some routine maintenance when I said to her, "You're a handsome sailing bitch, and if I had you to do over, the *only* thing I would change is your interior." And suddenly, there it was—the crux of the problem in full focus! She was fast, easily handled, and an excellent sea boat that *more* than fulfilled my performance expectations; however, her interior—for my family—was about the most unsuitable plan that could be envisioned.

It was the little things that got on my nerves while sailing, such as Jean yelling at the boys to quit dangling their feet over the stove or get out of the companionway. Or, we would sit down to dinner and someone would have to use the head, so the rest of us had to get up from one side of the table to provide a passageway, wait five minutes, then turn back to what *had* been a hot meal. There was also the lack for privacy for Karen who was in her modest teenage stage.

Upon going down into the forward cabin, the projecting galley counter required one to sidestep a half pace to proceed forward—not difficult, but bothersome. The cargo hold had become nothing more than a "catch-all." But the after cabin was the real thorn in my side. That popular-with-the-uninitiated danged double berth, and the even worse chart table that faced athwartship, had to go! Let me back up a bit. A double berth is great in port, but on a cruise or at sea, there is no body support for one person. Our double berth was difficult to make up besides. One had to get *on* the berth to tuck in the outside edge. Also, at anchor, at my time of life, it frequently becomes necessary for me to get up at night for a short turn on deck, and this does nothing but disturb Jean. Further, it was just not wide enough. Fifty-one inches sounds good, but I am 22″ across the shoulders which means I usually occupy at least half of the berth except when tossing and turning, and then I take up two-thirds. Finally, I knew better than to build a chart table that way, but I did, and in use it was nearly impossible to keep a chart from skidding off the table, along with the pencils, dividers, parallel rules and books.

So, in December 1970, I brought *Gazelle* into the cove with the idea of refinishing her and putting her on the market. My thoughts were not on a new boat any more than usual, other than the idea that "the next one will have to be a bit longer." That evening, this line of thought led to some calculation of cost. What I had thought was a fair market value for *Gazelle* would not duplicate her, much less build a larger boat! I had attributed the increase in cost of her sister ship, *Migrant*, built later, partly to inflation and partly to her engines. So, I went over the old invoices for both boats. I found that some items amounted to just pennies and some to just a few dollars, but all items together added up to several thousand dollars. Now, four years later, I discovered that to build *Gazelle* again would cost about $40,000, ready for sea! Of course, I could build a new hull through the corporation for less than that, and then do the interior myself away from the yard charges, but that would take another two years, and at the rate things were going, it seemed that the cost would increase another 20%.

In the yard, several changes had to be made—a new fitting-out wharf was needed and the launching railway had to be extended. We completed both of these jobs in early January, 1971. I then warped *Gazelle* in and did the only thing possible: "If thy hand offend thee, chop it off." I took a sledge hammer to the interior of *Gazelle*. Before the first blow, I could only recall that I had spent a thousand hours putting it in. But with the second blow, I began to think how nice it was going to be when it was rebuilt. I think Jean was somewhat appalled, and even suggested that maybe we could do the new interior in stages. But I would have none of that. I found that I could leave the area from the water closet forward alone, as it could easily be modified. Anyway, that area had worked pretty well so there was no reason to change it.

Here, in the lower end of the Chesapeake Bay, we do not haul our boats in the winter as there is seldom enough ice to do any damage. Some may think that to even consider rebuilding the interior of a boat while she is afloat borders on folly. This need not be the case as, with a little forethought during construction, level lines can be established, and in a total rebuilding task such as I was

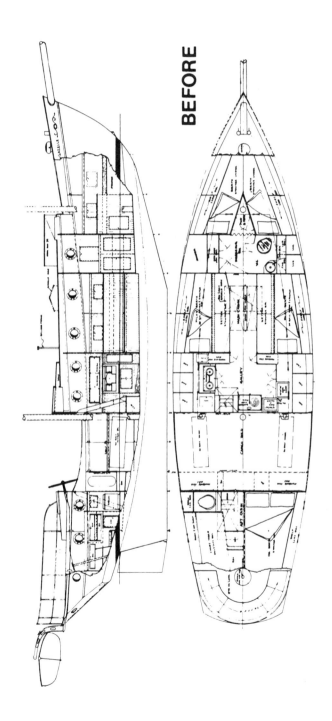

BEFORE

undertaking, it is easy to re-establish the level lines on which to work. Once the major structures such as bulkheads have been rebuilt and the new lines re-established, it is no more difficult working afloat than it is on land. In fact, it is probably easier as you don't have to climb up and down a ladder from the shop floor to the deck every time you want to get on or off the boat. It *is* a bit inconvenient if one is using shop tools to do much of the mill work, and the walking back and forth seems to equal a dozen miles a day. However, almost all of the interior rebuilding was done just with an electric drill, saber saw, and hand tools; I had power on the dock.

In the water closet forward, we rebuilt the basin into a cabinet, producing more storage space for soap, toilet paper, etc. In the forward cabin, the sea rails on the berths were cut down. When the children were smaller, higher sea rails were necessary to keep them in their bunks; however, now they are older and the difficulty of getting over the high sea rails begins to pose a problem. Nothing else in their cabin was altered other than framing the opening to the chain locker and installing a door to give that feature a more finished look and make it more functional.

The entire overhead of the hull was next insulated with a marine type fiberglass board. Its purpose was not to hold in the heat or keep out the cold or to control condensation, although it does all these jobs, but merely to dampen the noise of the children on the deck. It has helped considerably.

All of the changes to this point had done nothing but lower *Gazelle* even deeper forward, although the hull was gradually going down by the stern. Now the after cabin had some controlling factors that limited any new layout. Probably the most important was the bracket supporting the rudder post flared out to port and starboard at such angles that it was impossible to make the berths as wide as I would have liked without burning out and rewelding this supporting bracket. The berths could have been 2″ or 3″ wider with only minor additional modifications, but they are comfortable as they are now constructed. One surprising thing was the weight of wood I used rebuilding our cabin. Under the berths there is a series of lockers, shelves and bins, some opening in front of each berth, others accessible below the mattresses. The area between the berths (at the foot) and abaft the rudder post was converted to a shelf that holds the Tiny Tot stove, and below this is additional locker space.

In this cabin alone we probably doubled the storage capacity, and the accessibility to it is vastly improved. Between the berths and *forward* of the rudder post where we originally had a small radio shelf, we now have a larger and more useful shelf *plus* a settee that had doubled in size so that the two of us can sit there in comfort. This may not seem like much, but before this, one of us had to sit on the toilet top or in a berth while the other sat on the settee. Now there is room for two adults to dress or undress at the same time.

The lighting in our cabin was greatly improved by adding two kerosene lamps at the after end of the radio shelf. The toilet was already installed and I could see little point in changing its location. It was a little cramped, but is functional and that's all we cared about. I did add a folding wash basin over the toilet. With the new single berths being moved outboard, we now had a wide passageway into the old cargo hold. This change also shortened up the two small hanging lockers so they are now easier to use. Opposite the toilet and for the same width as the bulkhead to the passageway is a chart table, located at the head of the starboard berth. Below this chart table are chart shelves, and below them is an area which will hold our scuba tanks and diving gear. Karen, our 14-year-old daughter, and I, are both certified divers. Jean is well on her way to passing the tests, but has not completed all of them. However, all of us dive and snorkel, and at long last we have a proper area in which to stow this gear.

Well, my beloved cargo hold got the biggest change of all! One day in May, when all of the equipment was finally aboard the hull, we fabricated the engine bed, carried it down to the hull and temporarily fitted and checked it. Next we bolted it to the engine room bulkhead. It was notched over the existing floors and fitted very smoothly against the hull shell for the last 8" or 9" of its length. The following morning at low tide, the 10 hp Sabb diesel was moved on planks and rollers down to the wharf and on board. With the main halyard, we dropped her below and then, with a block and falls hooked onto one of the deck beams, she was eased into position. Everyone got off the boat and made observations from various points on shore. Sure enough, there she was, exactly in trim. I don't think she was "out" by more than a millimeter. I guess *Gazelle* knew that she would have an engine someday, although I would have given her a good argument on that point three years ago! True, she had a few more items to go aboard, but I felt these would be rather evenly distributed, such as water and fuel—although fuel is not a big factor as we have only a 12-gallon tank.

There were some awkward moments in doing the hook-up of the engine. Most of the instructions were quite clear, except that they were literal translations from Norwegian. I was finally able to obtain the original Norwegian booklet and found the missing diagrams that were so badly needed. What did not make sense were the very robust cable heads that were supplied for the remote controls. They

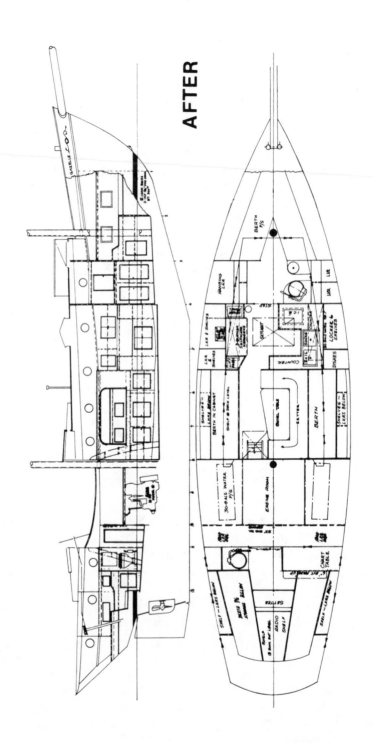

AFTER

had beautiful chrome handles and all bronze fittings. In this country, we certainly would have put them where they could be seen—that is, on the outside. But, no—I found that they were supposed to be installed below decks and out of sight. What a waste!

For an engine, I picked probably one of the few made in the world that does everything that an engine *should* do˙ and is still within my undestanding. Believe me, when it comes to mechanical things such as engines, this is very limited. I have, in my lifetime, seen enough of electronics to never want them aboard a boat. I have had trouble with starting engines, starter gears, and starter motors to know that they can be and usually are a source of one problem after the other, especially after a few years on the engine. So, I happily selected a hand-starting model—which has never yet let me down. The engine is a one-cylinder, four-cycle Sabb, made in Norway for fishermen. It produces 10 hp, and drives an 18″ controllable pitch propeller, and at full rpm the wheel turns 900 rpm.

While we had *Gazelle* up on the ways to install the engine, I decided to change her paint system to epoxies. So, we sandblasted her down to bare metal and refinished her up to the rails, applying coal tar based epoxies below the waterline, and bottom paint.

After relaunching she was still not ready to sail and our vacation cruise was fast approaching. As a compromise, we just sanded and varnished the forward cabin but left all the trim and the varnishing of the after cabin until some time in the future. The first week of our vacation was spent getting her ready for sea—putting stores aboard, connecting up the piping, conducting engine dock trials and rebending the sails.

The first day of our cruise we spent making engine sea trials. Happily, the engine installation has lived up to my expectations. It ran smoothly because of its counter-balance on the inside, with about the same amount of vibration one might expect from a four-cylinder diesel. With no wind at full rpm, we were able to get 7.15 knots with the current and 6.95 knots against the current. Unfortunately, this particular speed coincides with the structure of the steel hull to give a vibration node which, while not unpleasant to us does rattle the compass. By trying various rpm's we found the best setting—750 on the propeller, which is 1500 on the engine, at which rpm we get about 5.5 knots in smooth water, no wind, which is as much as we need.

Have I had any trouble with the engine? No, not with the engine. But I must admit that there are times that I wish I had stuck by my principles and not installed it. Now, *Gazelle* is just a wee bit more sluggish in light weather. It *does* make a difference to sailing performance whether the propeller is straight up and down or athwartships. And, I did hate to see our documentation papers changed from "sailing vessel" to "oil screw." What little the engine is used, the noise does not bother me. The big cargo hold which has become an engine room is still spotless. You could safely eat off the hull. The engine is equipped with a bilge pump, and by proper piping I have been able to take raw water from overboard and pump it up to deck level where I can hose down (which sure beats heaving the bucket), and I can wash my anchor chain and anchors off as they come up out of the muck. Other than for demonstration purposes, the engine is seldom used. In fact, as I write in the fall of 1971, this season she has less than 25 hours running time, and 20 hours of that was on our vacation cruise during flat calms. The Sabb is quite an economical little thing. She burns approximately a third of a gallon per hour at cruising speed, so little, in fact, that it's embarrassing to go to a fuel dock so we carry five gallons in a gerry can, so we never go into a dock. That's fine with us as we all prefer to anchor out all the time. Even our ten-year-old, Kevin, finds no trouble at all in hand-cranking the engine, much to his delight. Unfortunately for me, *he* likes engines!

The new interior arrangement has worked out even better than expected. The diagnosis was correct, and my major surgery was the cure. Without ruining the hull, we have increased its utility greatly in all respects, yet we have not diminished her capability as a blue water cruiser. She is *still* simple; we still do not have a central electrical system; we *still* use kerosene lights; we *still* use Hot Shot batteries for instant light and reading lights at the berths, and that sparingly. We have room now to carry a couple of hundred books with us; we do have a greater degree of privacy; and I believe that *Gazelle's* fitness for blue water cruising has been enhanced by the modifications made on deck and by the increased ventilation below. In holing up for hurricane Donna, we found that we had adequate ventilation.

The dinghy is still something of a problem, and I am still not particularly happy with it hung over the stern in davits, but it is *a* solution, and whether or not that will be a good dinghy location at sea is still undetermined. *Gazelle's* sister, *Migrant*, reported only a couple of occasions where rogue seas from astern broke over the after deck, so I am hopeful that the dinghy can stay there. *Migrant* carries hers, a smaller model, on the main cabin trunk.

I think it might be useful here to note that while *Gazelle* has not made the ocean passages we had hoped to make, *Migrant* has, sailing approximately 17,000 miles in 15 months. She cruised to the Bras d'Or Lakes in Nova Scotia, then south and through the

Bahamas to Jamaica, Cartegena, Colombia and Cape San Blas Islands, passed through the Panama Canal and on to the Galapagos, from the Galapagos to the Marquesas, the Marquesas to the Hawaiian Islands, and from there to Bellingham, Washington. Her best day's run was 202 nautical miles. Her two best passages were from the Galapagos to the Marquesas, a little over 3000 miles in 500 hours of sailing, and from the Marquesas to Hawaii at an average of 6 knots. Her owner, Dick Johnson, told me his use of the engine has been minimal. At sea, I think it consisted of only 35 minutes, *total*. Considering the length of the voyage, it hardly paid for its own weight as ballast. However, coming across the Pacific high from Hawaii, Dick ran his engine for 17 hours to work out of the calms. He was then hove-to under bare poles for some 17 hours, and weathered a gale for three days. So I would say that, all in all, *Migrant* has more than fulfilled the original requirement as a fast ocean sailer. Her best weekly run for seven days, noon-to-noon, was 1145 miles, with a "family" crew—the owner, his wife, and three children. I had originally thought she would reel off many 125 mile days and that this would be close to her average, but I was too conservative in my estimate, and at sea she is closer to 140 to 142 miles per day. I won't complain about this at all.

So, for the present at least, and probably for some years to come, *Gazelle* is a fine vessel for our purposes, requiring very few major improvements. She still needs a few small items such as a writing table that hinges down from the chart table, which will make writing up the log easier. I am sure that, from time to time, other things will suggest themselves and will be added. But *Gazelle* is my boat, and she now suits me just fine. I would not recommend her as the ideal boat for everyone, as each person has different requirements.

If there is a moral, conclusion, or lesson to be derived from this experience of rebuilding *Gazelle*, it must be that before putting a loved one on the auction block for minor faults, it may be wise to regroom and rebuild her, and then happily enjoy the result.

On Using the Beaufort Scale

Whenever I hear anyone estimating and describing wind and sea conditions, I am appalled at their apparent abandonment of the Beaufort Scale. Not only is it accurate, but the Beaufort Scale is descriptive and deserves to be learned and used on all cruising vessels to the exclusion of other "lubberly" terminology now employed.

The Table, included below, is the one I learned many years ago from sailors who began their careers before the turn of the century. This Scale description has been changed many times during the last 70 years, but it seems clear that the old descriptions are vivid and more meaningful than today's .

Also included is the velocity of the wind (in knots) and the force (in pounds per square foot) that a given wind produces on the sails. For the technically-minded, vector analysis would be required to modify what is shown to allow for hull speed, but the stated pressure gives an idea of the flogging of the sails when coming about.

Incorporated in the table is a recommended amount of sail and the approximate speed in knots for each wind force when close-hauled (which I define as close as the vessel will sail and make progress), and broad reaching with the wind on the quarter. The speed given in these two columns is based on a 36' waterline vessel. For example, in Force 3 winds, the description would be "gentle breeze; the foam has a glossy appearance but is not yet white."

Close-hauled, one would carry working sails and topsails, and would attain a speed of 5 to 6 knots. Broad-reaching, one would carry working sails, topsails, and other light sails such as a fisherman, a flying jib, squaresails, etc., and would have a speed of 6 to 7 knots. This, of course, would depend on how much sail could be raised. The velocity of the wind would be 15.6 knots, which would result in a pressure of 1.2 lbs. per sq. ft. of sail area exposed.

As the seas increase, the ability to point decreases. In the extreme at Force 8, the vessel must make good to windward only a quarter point to be included in this category. Many vessels cannot do this. Above Force 9, we are concerned with survival, and it is impossible to lay down hard and fast rules as each vessel has her own peculiarities. The competency and judgement of her crew are also factors.

Generally speaking, a vessel with a deep forefoot will lie to a sea anchor about 5 points off the wind and drift square with the wind. A shallow-forefoot vessel will lie about 9 points off the wind and her drift will be square with the wind, wheel amidships. A vessel with no forefoot will seldom lay closer than 12 points and should, therefore, be brought stern-to and set a sea anchor, drogue or warps over the stern. It is well to remember that, stern-to, the vessel must be kept moving or she will be overtaken and pooped by the seas. Usually, from .5 to .8 times the square root of the waterline is the most comfortable speed; or, in the case of the 36-footer, from 3 to 5 knots (.5 x 6 = 3.0 knots; .8 x 6 = 4.8 knots.) Sailing too fast is an invitation to broaching. Surfing in a racing vessel is possible with a large crew; however, it is unwise on the average cruising vessel with her small crew.

Having experienced hurricanes and typhoons in ships as well as small vessels, I have no wish to repeat these experiences. The wise master will heave-to a little too early rather than attempt it too late. As a last resort, all running rigging could be brought down and sails unbent, and booms lashed to the deck to reduce windage. When hove-to, if the vessel forereaches, the wheel is put up; if she is making some sternway, then the rudder must be amidships.

Each master can apply the accompanying Beaufort Scale directly and need only modify his speed in knots. Properly canvased, any vessel, from say 25' to 75' of waterline length, can utilize this table. Speed will vary as the square root of 36 is to the square root of the new vessel's waterline times the speed given. This factor will be multiplied by the speed given in columns 4 and 5 to arrive at the new speed for another vessel being considered.

To allow for the differences in vector because of the vessel's speed, the table can also be used for approximating the additional pressure on the sails due to being close-hauled or broad-reaching. A rough rule of thumb would be, in this case, to use pounds per square foot at Force 4 for close-hauled, and pounds per square foot for Force 2 for broad-reaching.

The velocities given are "flat plate pressure"—wind blowing at right angles to the sail—no movement. One must realize that for any given force the description and state of the sea are constants. The direction in which the vessel is sailing does not affect the state of the sea nor the true wind. It affects only the apparent pounds per square foot and the apparent velocity of the wind. This is the reason why one vessel, close-hauled, may consider the wind blowing a gale; whereas, to another vessel, running, it is just a nice sailing breeze.

The Beaufort Wind Scale, Based on a 36' Waterline Cruising Vessel

Beaufort Number	Description of Sea	State of Sea	Close Hauled	Broad Reach	Velocity In Knots	Force In LBS/Sq Ft
0	Calm	Smooth, mirror-like.	All sail; 0-1 knot.	All sail; 0-1.5 knots.	0-2.6	.03
1	Light Air	Smooth, small wavelets.	All sail; 1-2 knots.	All sail; 2-3.5 knots.	6.9	.23
2	Light Breeze	Small waves, crests breaking	All sail; vessel heels moderately. 3-4 knots.	All sail; 4-6 knots.	11.3	.62
3	Gentle Breeze	Foam has glossy appearance; not yet white.	Working sail and topsails. 5-6 knots.	Working sails; topsails & light sails; 6-7 knots.	15.6	1.20
4	Moderate Breeze	Larger waves, many "white horses."	Working sail only; Lt Displacement vessels reef. 6-7 knots.	Full working sail & topsails; Lt Displ. hand topsails; 7-8 knots.	20	1:90
5	Stiff Breeze	Waves pronounced; long white foam crests.	All vessels reef; Lt Displacement double reef; 5-6 knots.	Working sails only; 8-9 knots.	24.3	2.90

Rules given for handling a vessel at sea must be modified for existing circumstances and conditions.

6	Fresh Breeze	Large waves, white foam crests all over.	Deep reefs; 3-4 knots.	Hvy Displ, small reefs; Lt Displ, deep reefs; 8-9 knots.	29.5	4.20
7	Very Fresh Breeze	Sea heaps up; wind blows foam in streaks.	Hvy Displ, deep reefs; Lt Dis, min. working sail. 2-3 knots.	Deep reefs in largest sail; 8-9 knots.	34.7	5.9
9	Strong Gale	Foam blown in dense streaks.	Lying ahull; sea anchor or drogue out; side drift.	Run off--under bare poles and warps. 3-5 knots.	48.1	11.50
10	Very Strong Gale	High waves; long overhanging crests; Lg. foam patches.	Lying ahull; sea anchor or drogue.	Run off--bare poles & warps; 3-5 knots; speed too great; danger of broaching.	56.4	15.5
11	Violent Gale	High waves	Lie to sea anchor.	Bare poles; sea anchor, warps, drogue; vessel must be slowed down.	65.1	20.6
12	Hurricane; Typhoon	Streaking foam; Spray in air.	Lie to sea anchor.	Lie to sea anchor.	78.1	29.6

On Privacy

Even people who totally subscribe to "togetherness" will occasionally require complete privacy. At sea, space and distance are at a premium; therefore, it becomes necessary to plan into the arrangement a space where each individual can go without having his or her privacy invaded without consent. A place where he or she can be "alone"—at least to a limited degree.

In the past, in the present, and I assume also in the future, about the best place for privacy is each crewman's berth. So, incorporated into this sleeping area must be lockers and shelves to stow not only the body but personal effects such as clothes, books, camera, toilet articles, mementoes, and other sundries that are not common property. All other spaces must be shared equally in a small cruiser. This immediately rules out settee berths, dinette berths, "hot bunk-

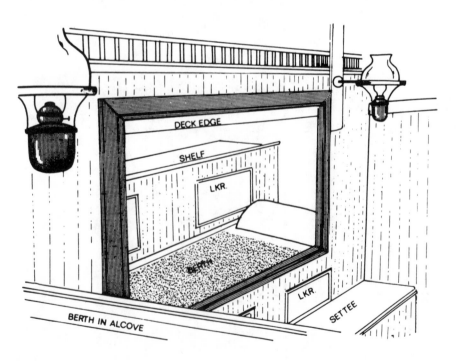

ing," or any other dodge that gives a multi-purpose to a berthing area.

Most ocean cruisers are much too small to allow each crew member a space for a sea chest. Indeed, they are no longer necessary as crews no longer hop from one vessel to another. The berth should be arranged for maximum stowage, and one good arrangement is to have a shelf run the full length of the berth. If there is enough vertical room above it—over 12"—then a small locker with shelves within it could be located at each end of this shelf, and the area *below* the shelf arranged into lockers with at least three, if not four, compartments between the mattress and the hull. If possible, each berth should be provided with its own reading light.

This is not much to ask for; however, even this minimum often makes for a happier crew. If the berth can be curtained off, so much the better. Elsewhere, the vessel (within natural limitations) should be laid out for communal living with the minimum necessary space for the crew to move fore-and-aft through the vessel without disturbing the cook or navigator.

On Galleys

The foc'sle is still the most economical space to locate the galley, and a galley so placed has the maximum usable space for the minimum expenditure of cabin sole. However, it takes a cook with a cast-iron stomach to prepare proper sea-going meals up forward, so I doubt that many will select this location. Let me say, however, that in most vessels the foot of the companionway is *equally objectionable*. For years, I have listened to the propaganda that the primary reason for locating the galley aft was to let the cook converse with the helmsman. I suggest that reason is more imagined than real. First, it would be a disjointed conversation indeed, if each is concentrating on his own duties. Second, in rain or heavy weather, who can hear? Third, we have already established that a good ocean cruiser should be able to sail herself, so this shoots one more hole in the argument.

I suggest that the saloon should be aft and the galley be located where the saloon usually is. Then, those coming below will not be in the cook's way and, above all, the cook is in a position where he or she will be least bothered by down-drafts and rain coming through the hatch. Put a skylight over the galley and locate a turbine vent in the after end of the cabin trunk, and you will have good ventilation for the cook.

Another often-forgotten fact is that galleys situated in the widest part of the hull are subject to the greatest amount of transverse motion, just as those in the foc'sle are subject to the greatest amount of pitching. So moving the galley just seven feet forward often makes it possible to have more hot meals in heavy weather, not to mention leaving the widest part of the hull for that center of below-decks living, the saloon.

On Interior Arrangement and Stowage

Adequate stowage is the first requirement of a vessel's interior, whether it be bodies, stores, spares, water, fuel, sails or any of the hundreds of other items that make up an ocean cruiser. Stowage should remain foremost in the mind of the designer, builder *and* owner. After years of facing this problem, I find it difficult to allow for all of this without at least 10′ of hull per person being accommodated. In an ocean cruiser without a cockpit, it may be possible to reduce the rate to 7′ per person provided there is an *even* number of berths.

The *Luxury* is the settee—the stowage area below it is the *necessity*. In every instance, the maximum amount of space must be utilized for stores, but not at the expense of hindering vessel maintenance. In other words, stowage areas must be accessible, but the hull over, under, inboard and outboard of such stowage areas must also be accessible for cleaning, painting and repair.

The trick is not how many cubby holes and clever lockers can be devised and built in, but how many can be *conveniently* added—in combination with or continuation of another necessary design feature. As with a deck box used as a catch-all for deck gear, and also serving as a ventilator and light board, so many other structures within the hull can serve a dual purpose. For example, berths are often placed over a water tank. Raising the berth further, or lowering the tank, permits a storage area. Other examples which come to mind are a chart table over an icebox, a work bench over a fuel tank in the engine room, a forward berth over a chain locker, etc. All cruisers should have a work bench, vise, carpenter's tools and lumber as well as metal, leather, sail repair kit, and wire- and rope-splicing equipment aboard.

Did I forget to mention the bilges? In some vessels, there is a vast amount of space available there, and it can best be utilized for stowing canned goods, but only after the labels have been removed and the cans marked. This is *not* only because they might fall off, for the bilges in our steel *Gazelle* are usually dusty—but because cans from warehouses or grocery stores often have cockroach nits in the glue of the paper. It is crowded enough on the small cruiser without having those fellows as shipmates!

On Dinghies

If there is a thorn in the side of the small vessel ocean voyager, it is probably the dinghy. When a dinghy is needed, it is very, very useful, but when it is not, it is horrid.

At lengths below 30′, I guess about the only really practical dinghy to have aboard the vessel is the inflatable type. This allows it to be stowed off the deck, which is limited in a smaller vessel. At 40′, with two cabin trunks and if adequate design work has been done, it can be stowed athwartships between the two cabins. On top of either cabin trunk is possible, too, but it certainly makes reefing an inconvenience. Even here there would be an advantage with an inflatable except that most of them row like a garbage scow.

Folding boats are good as are kyacks, but really are in the same category as the inflatable. It takes quite a bit of time to set one up, and this is a real bother if you are anchoring every night on a cruise.

When a vessel gets above 45′, vessel size makes possible stowing a dinghy on board and out of the way. With any depth of hull, the dinghy can stand in chocks on the fore and aft centerline of the deck, as most of the deck can be flush. In shoaler hulls, it still must be stowed athwartships. At 50′ or so, it is possible to hang one in davits over the stern. I am not altogether happy with this arrangement on smaller boats as it is possible to lose the dinghy at sea under extreme conditions, but it certainly is convenient in coastwise cruising.

When choosing a dinghy, a pram has the most room for the smallest length. Of all the prams, the Auray fisherman's dinghy is the best for rowing and to take the surf, but it is not practical in lengths of less than 9′.

The conventional round-bottom dinghy with a sharp bow usually rows the best. But in all cases, anything less than 10′ in length is not a great joy to row for any distance. Unfortunately, the better rowing dinghies usually exceed 12′ in length which is much too long for small ocean cruisers. Under no circumstances should the minimum freeboard (loaded) be less than around 8″.

It is a snare and a delusion to consider a dinghy a lifeboat. I cannot conceive of abandoning a sound hull at sea and jumping into a dinghy. As a true lifeboat—well, I would think this use would come only if sinking when there was no other alternative. Fortunately, most catastrophes happen close to shore, and I would just as soon have a good life jacket.

Cruising Lockers

"The time has come, the Walrus said, to speak of many things; of shoes and ships and sealing wax, and . . ."

I have frequently been asked what equipment and ship's stores should be carried for ocean cruising, and for permanent living aboard. According to whom I am speaking, or perhaps more accurately, based on how I feel that particular day, my answer ranges from what one *only* needs to everything one might *ever* need. I think this wide variance stems from whether I am thinking of living aboard, or just cruising. Of course, anyone cruising *is* living aboard, but many people who live aboard do not really cruise.

A vessel circumnavigating requires many times the volume of stores, spare parts, and tools needed say, for a fortnight's cruise on the Chesapeake Bay. When the vessel serves for permanent living aboard plus short cruising, then her requirements will fall between the world cruiser and the vacation cruiser. Many owners of weekend cruisers, when visiting an ocean cruiser, are awestruck by the vast amount of spare parts, equipment, sails and tools carried aboard, and the high state of maintenance they observe. Their most-often-heard remarks include: "If my boat had that much stuff aboard, she'd sink!" or "With all that gear abord, he ought to have a cargo hold," and sometimes, but not often, "Oh, well, I guess he can afford it."

The truth of the matter is that, in most cases, the cruising owner can ill afford to be without all the spare parts and equipment aboard for the safety of his vessel and crew, as his chances of making his ports and his voyage are dependent upon his ability to keep his vessel in first-class condition, and to be self-sustaining.

It is difficult to conceive that a cruising man would deprive his vessel of any spares or equipment that can logically be carried aboard, for cruising vessels are—often for long periods—out of touch with not only other vessels but *any* outside help. Even if help were available, the distance away might be so great as to make assistance impossible.

For coastwise cruising, the volume of spares can be limited sharply, although there should be enough rigging aboard, for instance, to replace the longest shroud or stay that might be damaged. There should also be the right tools to accomplish these repairs in the minimum time. Since the vessel is sailing coastwise, major items of equipment could be purchased in many ports, or probably could be obtained by mail in a week or so. However, I feel that the risk of even a 24-hour delay justifies keeping a complete set of spares aboard. Even for short "foreign" voyages such as to the Bahamas, Virgin Islands, West Indies and South or Central America, any vessel, like the long-distance vessel, should be able to handle any repair short of sinking, and this includes many repairs that would lead to sinking if left unattended. This equipment should include major replacement of standing and running rigging, blocks, extra ground tackle, extra planking stock (in the case of a wooden vessel), fastenings, steering gear parts (if a worm steerer is not used), portlight glass, caulking—in fact, everything that would be necessary to sufficiently repair the vessel. Thus, anyone doing serious cruising, besides being a sailor, also should be a boatbuilder, mechanic, electrician, navigator, sailmaker, rigger, doctor, lawyer, pilot, and philosopher.

Bo'sun's Locker

For want of a better term, I suppose we can call the place where all these things are stored the "bo'sun's locker" although under this heading we must also include several other categories covering other jobs done by the bo'sun. Where the bo'sun's locker is located is not too important—I have used almost every location, including the w. c. Through the years one of my objections to an engine, aside from its own complications, is that it uses up an excellent location for the bo'sun's locker, or for a work bench and rigging shop. *With* an engine, possible locations for the bo'sun's locker include the lazarette, the foc'sle or forepeak, under the companionway steps, in a deck box, in several ditty bags on which the different categories of equipment have been stenciled, in a bin, under a bin, under a settee, in shelves in the dressing room, or at the bottom of a hanging locker. On *Gazelle* we have no cockpit so below the bridge deck is the engine room (former cargo hold) where the engine is flanked by bins, work benches, lockers, tool drawers and spare parts lockers.

There is one *other* stipulation for the bo'sun's locker: It must be divided into various categories. Then, without searching or fumbling, it is just a matter of taking the right bag, locker, box, or whatever the container is to have the right tool at the right moment at one's fingertips. One of the most exasperating experiences is to be working on deck and, needing one item, have to go below and rummage through five lockers to find it—and maybe *not* find it. Even worse is to spend an hour looking for an item needed on a 10-minute job. Worse still is to have to borrow from another vessel. When a vessel is kept shipshape by proper stowage of required equipment, repairs can be made in any emergency—even at night—with minimum cost in time and effort. In short, more time should be spent learning to be an able seaman than a fashionable owner.

Bo'sun's Box

Many years ago when I owned a 21-foot sloop, I made a bo'sun's box and used it on that and several subsequent vessels. It was just high enough to make a good seat and was often incorporated as part of a settee. It stowed under the companionway in one later vessel, serving as both seat and step. This box was both small and handy, but took two men to lift it. It held a large collection of tools and was so complete that 99% of the time nothing more was required from ashore. The top was made in the form of a bo'sun's chair.

There are a number of lockers aboard a vessel which the designer finds it difficult to designate on the arrangement plan at the very beginning, but which should be located and fitted just as soon as the owner is accustomed to the vessel. It would be nice to think that they could be predetermined, but this is rarely possible. They are additive lockers and must be built into the vessel before she is a proper cruiser. These lockers are: sail locker, deck locker, rigging locker, hull locker, personal and miscellaneous locker, slop chest, bonded stores locker, abandon-ship locker, paint locker, engine and mechanical locker.

Handy-Billy

One important piece of gear that should certainly be on board, that might be included in any of several lockers, is a "handy-billy." This device consists of a single and a double metal block, each with hooks at the ends, and both rove with about 100 feet of 3/8″ dacron rope. As its name implies, the handy-billy is used wherever a little extra help is needed for lifting heavy weights or setting up rigging. I can remember one occasion when one was even sufficient for stepping a jury-rigged spar after a dismasting at sea.

Sail Locker

The sail locker should contain a large variety of needles, about a dozen of the most useful sizes plus extras. The points would be set into a cork and then put in a plastic bottle filled with oil to prevent rust. In a separate bottle, store additional needles with blunted points, for roping. Both of these bottles are wrapped in light canvas so that if the oil spills it will not soil anything. There should be a lump of beeswax, sail twine (both waxed and unwaxed), two sizes of marlin, three sizes of grommets with grommet punches and sets, scissors, knife, razor blade, two palms (roping and seaming), a bench hook, spare jib snaps, tape, and about a dozen precut sail patches, tightly rolled, from 6" square to 2' square.

Deck Locker

The deck locker and the hull locker sometimes become interchangeable when the tools are shifted from one to the other, but they should contain *at least* the following: several screw drivers, regular pliers, needle-nose pliers, nippers, scraper blades (made from the best saw that can be bought and cut up into squares with the edges knurled), two putty knives, a caulking iron, box of tacks, two or three dozen screws (assorted sizes), ditto for bolts, a twist auger (I usually make my own), a Yankee screwdriver, a Yankee drill, 4-1b. hammer, claw hammer, two ball peen hammers, set of wood chisels, set of cold chisels, several rasps, a file, wetstone, bungs of different sizes, caulking cotton, lap links, split links, small can of Dutch Boy white lead, hacksaw and blades, hatchet, a broad hatchet (not the Boy Scout type), two block planes, spokeshave, drawknife, two handsaws and a dovetail saw. Also, it's a good idea to include a jackknife in *each* locker.

Rigging Locker

In the rigging locker we should find marlin (several balls in different weights), and a marlin spike—not the round type, but something like the type I make (see sketch). I've often wondered why some manufacturer does not make such a marlin spike since it does the job of splicing wire so much better. Using "my" type, one merely inserts the point, pushes it in as far as necessary and gives it a half-turn. This lays open the wire with more than enough room to lay through the strand. With a round model, especially in larger sizes, it's often necessary to use two, but with the Colvin type, splicing wire becomes *almost* a pleasure.

Next there are shackles, two dozen of each of the most common sizes, plus a half dozen each of the odd sizes. There should be three fids of different sizes, seizing wire, extra sheaves, sheave pins, cotter pins, snap shackles, a couple of spare metal blocks, and a couple of complete turnbuckles. When a turnbuckle breaks and is replaced, the surviving parts can be cannibalized as spares. Also needed are a pair of crescent wrenches, the most commonly used size of open-end wrench, one small pipe wrench, one medium pipe wrench, several small rods (1/4", 5/16", 3/8", 1/2") of different lengths, parrel beads, copper rivets, a handful of tapered plugs and a couple of bull's-eyes.

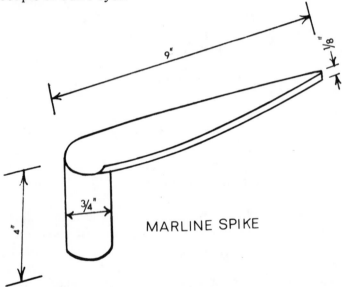

MARLINE SPIKE

Stowed somewhere on board should be sufficient wire to replace all of the standing rigging on the *mainmast*. In the lazarette should be an additional 250' of 5/8" nylon rope for kedging off when grounded or for dragging a warp when running off in heavy seas. There should be sufficient running rigging to replace the halyards on both masts and, since the sheets and halyards should be the same diameter, they would be interchangable.

I still make it a practice to end-for-end sheets and halyards at least once each season. When *Gazelle* is off soundings, I frequently change them during the voyage, how often depending on how careful I've been about preventing chafe. Of course, after several end-for-endings and shortenings, these lines become too short and are demoted to the next shortest line for which they will serve.

Dacron line does not make good baggy wrinkles, but does make good fenders. I must admit that occasionally I still buy a coil of manila just for baggy wrinkles, and I confess to still liking manila for many other uses aboard. It makes excellent "small stuff" and can be spliced, tapered and worked into many fancy items that are difficult with dacron.

Personal and Miscellaneous Locker

This one should include a non-electric soldering iron, solder (both cored and plain), solder paste, stove parts, assorted gaskets, neoprene sheets for making gaskets, a toilet repair kit, lamp wicks, aspirin box with assorted change, paper, pencils, a cheap pocket watch, matches, a mirror, and a lot of little odds and ends that seem to accumulate like junk. This locker has to be cleaned out periodically in order to keep it closed.

Paint Locker

Another locker that should be specifically located in the hull is the paint locker. It should be a separate and well ventilated compartment, bin or locker. If this is impossible, at least locate it *away* from the engine room, cabin heaters and the galley, for the fumes from opened cans of paints and thinners are volatile. Depending on the size of the vessel, I usually choose between the forepeak or foc'sle, and the lazarette. In *Gazelle* the paint locker is in the bottom of a hanging locker. In recent years I have noticed many vessels don't carry paint with them when cruising but depend on purchasing it at the various ports along the way. It is quite easy to achieve a state of mind that will permit this type of cruising, for certainly paint does rob one of useful space. But each time I am about ready to leave the paint ashore, something happens to reaffirm my belief in absolute independence while cruising.

Bonded Stores Locker

The bonded stores locker is a requirement for foreign cruising. It is used for storing tobacco, liquor and other stores that are bought in bond for use outside the country, at sea. It is used and respected by almost all nations. The customs agent normally seals the locker while the vessel is in port, and a severe penalty is levied if it is broken open while in port. The tax on these items bought in bond is considerable, so this can constitute a large savings for the cruising owner.

Slop Chest

The slop chest is another locker omitted by some owners. On more than one occasion at sea I have blessed the foresight that led me to put one aboard. On commercial vessels the slop chest is a locker from which seamen can purchase oilskins, clothing, tobacco, candy and other small necessities and luxuries, and is required by law on most such vessels. On a cruising vessel, the slop chest should include some old clothing, old oilskins, extra sea boots, extra blankets, etc. to be used in an emergency. One can never tell when he may rescue someone from the water or take a sick or injured person from another vessel.

Abandon Ship Locker

Another locker which I consider essential but rarely see aboard a cruising vessel is the Emergency or Abandon-Ship Locker, to be used, obviously, if sunk or wrecked. I am not a Doomsday forecaster, and fortunately the majority of us will not experience these events in a lifetime of cruising, but one never knows—it could happen on the next voyage. We usually carry a few cans of lifeboat water and food, a sheath knife, a hatchet, a machete, waterproof matches, emergency first aid and medicine kit, and signal flares. This is the only portable locker aboard *Gazelle*.

Gadgets & Mechanical Aptitude

It is difficult to understand how so many yachtsmen can afford numerous gadgets for their vessels (which they seldom know how to use correctly) but cannot afford to buy a separate set of tools to be used only in the maintenance of the engine, auxiliary, and mechanical parts of the vessel. Further, why are such tools, if they are aboard, so often in a poor condition? In many auxiliaries I have inspected, the engine room has the appearance of being treated like a poor relative. If one puts a piece of equipment aboard, it deserves as much attention as the polished brass bell on deck which everyone can see. Perhaps one reason I can accept the "simplicity in cruising" that I find satisfying is that I make it a rule to take nothing aboard that I cannot maintain and repair myself.

Some may think I am a trained mechanic, but I am not—far

from it. In the case of our new diesel engine, I am able—from practice and a careful reading of the manual, to disassemble it and put it back together again. The same is true for the British Seagull we use on the dinghy. I have taken it apart several times and have replaced almost every part in the engine, and it works when I am finished. Knowing my equipment this way, it is no calamity when something goes wrong.

Also carried in the engine compartment and for the engine only are packing for the stuffing box, enough lube oil for several changes, spare parts and tools furnished with the engine by Sabb, and some extra tools which I found handy when I was installing the engine.

Nowadays, it is common to have a radio. Ours is a combination radio-direction-finder, which is a Heathkit. It is not too difficult to assemble and, with a little forethought and some advice from the factory plus the instruction booklet for assembling it and a few spares, it seems to stay in good working order. The taffrail log presents little problem in maintenance and is kept well-oiled and in its box most of the time.

With the above, I reach my zenith in equipment. Again I reflect on the pleasure of my early cruises compared with those of today, and there is really very little difference, for in cruising I have still tried to maintain simplicity in everything. My family and I are able to enjoy cruising without refrigeration and, as I have mentioned elsewhere, ice is merely a weekend luxury. We do not abhore the idea of kerosene in place of electric lights. My auxiliary is used as a convenience and not as a necessity. We are able to spend as many as 45 days at a time away from a dock and, if we carry out water in jugs to replenish our tanks, or catch rain water aboard, the time spent away from a dock could be indefinite, for we are also capable of beaching our vessel for cleaning and painting the bottom. Because of this simplicity, our ratio of enjoyment to maintenance is at a maximum as we can perform all maintenance that might be required.

As the amount of time in cruising surpasses the amount of time spent at a dock, the more important becomes the livability of the interior of the vessel; the more important it is to eliminate all makeshift arrangements; and the more important it is to increase the size and equipment of the various lockers. In any serious cruising, say six months to four or five years away from one's home port, the ability to be completely independent of boatyards, marinas, etc. becomes increasingly important.

Remember that cruising does not have to be a trek to the same old ports that everyone else visits, or even a great distance. There is still much pleasure to be found cruising into little-known harbors and coves if one is prepared for this approach, perhaps even more pleasure in these days of crowded waters. There's no finer feeling when departing on a cruise than to be able to say, even if only to yourself, "My vessel is ready in every respect, and I am, too, within the limits of my ability." And then, *go*!

On Water Tanks

When I was a boy, built-in water tanks were not universal, especially in small cruisers. We usually had a water butt on deck, forward of the cabin trunk, with a flap on top and a ladle attached by a lanyard. It was simple and foolproof if somewhat inconvenient. In those days, the galley was either in the foc's'le or at the forward end of the cabin; thus, on some vessels the owners could have running water in the galley and water closet by tapping the butt through a hole in the deck. Changing fashion made these tanks unsightly, and soon water tanks were put below decks, often piped to a small day tank of three-or four-gallon capacity, fitted between the cabin beams or in an overhead locker.

World War II brought the greatest changes, for this was the era of mass production; so the many small lockers in custom-built interiors gave way to the cheaper (and more "fashionable") bins, with very little joiner work. This required the use of pumps at each point where water was needed—usually just in the galley. Newcomers to boating had never been exposed to the old ways, and eventually water pressure systems came along which required electricity to achieve what Granddad did with gravity.

This is not to imply that everything old is necessarily best—only that some of the old ways are worth reinvestigation to determine if the new is *really* best. On *K'ung Fu-Tse*, I have a complete gravity system (with hot water as well) and Nature does most of the work. I must admit that the Chinese junk hull lends itself to the system, for under the after deck is a 20-gallon tank which is 4 feet above the galley sink and 3 feet above the aft wash basin. On deck over the galley there is a 15-gallon tank, painted black. We pump from our main water tanks to the aft tank for fresh water, and fill the black tank with sea water. The sun heats the water the black tank, which is filled by bucket each morning when the decks are washed down.

The best part, though, is that we purchased our two fixtures at a plumbing supply house for $4.00 and $12.00—all bronze with heavy chrome. These fixtures are standard so parts will be standard over most of the world.

So, while the convenience of the system or the availability of standard fittings may never have been considered by the old-timers, one must concede that the desire for running water did not force them to the opposite direction—pressure switches, batteries, electric wiring plus an engine to make it all function!

On Filtering Fuel

One can usually assume safely that in North America fuel received from a dock pump has been filtered and is free of the water, dirt and other things that clog injectors or carburetor jets. One can further assume that a vessel used in summer months need only take minimal precautions in these waters to guard against condensation within the tanks. But for permanent living aboard and foreign voyaging, this assumption can lull one into unnecessary mechanical failures.

Heating and cooling the engine room during winter operation of the vessel will cause condensation in the tanks. Also, when voyaging, it is possible to receive fuel from barrels and tanks that have been neglected or standing for many years and so may contain water, rust, dirt or—not infrequently—a mixture of other fuels such as lube or crude oil still in the barrel or tanks from a previous filling.

To avoid these hazards, for some years now I have used a multiple filtering system which, while not foolproof, at least minimizes the possiblity of dirty fuel. First, all fuel taken aboard is passed through a screened funnel into the main tank. From the main tank I pump through primary and secondary cartridge filters (paper elements) to a day tank that provides 12 hours (minimum) or 24 hours (maximum) fuel capacity. The bottom of this tank has a pot of two-cup capacity with a drain cock. Above the drain cock (but still *in* the cup) is a draw-off, leading by gravity to a second set of filters (again a primary and secondary cartridge). These are connected to the fuel filter on the engine which leads to the sediment bowl—thence to the engine. All of the filters have drain cocks; therefore, all fuel has eight opportunities to be cleaned before use. Even then, some junk may slip through.

How often does one run a line check? Well, it depends on weather, fuel source and frequency of engine use. The first pair of filters should be checked after taking on fuel, and then once every tenth day-tank filling. The day tank should be checked daily. The *last* set of filters should be checked monthly if the day tank is running clean, or weekly if the day tank is yielding water or other sediment.

Gravity-feed tanks are frowned upon as an improper installation and their use can be dangerous. One usually cannot obtain insurance with this installation, and the Coast Guard and other agencies become upset about openings out of the bottom of any fuel tanks. Since the majority of ocean voyagers cannot afford insurance—even if it were available—and inasmuch as we must operate under the most varied conditions, these facts and precations are a safety factor which, to my thinking, we should exercise for survival. However, the rule-makers neither comprehend nor recognize these facts.

This system permits one to bypass, say, a faulty fuel lift pump. There is one case when this system does not work well—when the diesel has a return fuel line that returns to the tank many times the amount of fuel actually consumed. In the tropics, the returning fuel is heated and eventually the hot fuel can cause the engine to starve. There are ways to cool such fuel, but it is usually best to return it to the main tank.

On Sailing Downwind

Inasmuch as I was born in the year of the Ox, it seems possible that I have inherited some of the bovine characteristics of that creature. In the past, the red flag of dogmatic or illogical statements affected me more than they do today. On occasion, however, some nautical statements still try my patience. One of these is that "the shortest route is the fastest route." This may be true applied to aircraft, but it is seldom true in ocean voyaging, when the more circuitous route is often not only the fastest, but the most pleasureable and practical.

Past experience has repeatedly convinced me that sailing closer than 5 points to the wind is miserable as well as tiring for the crew, and a long beat to windward is hard on the vessel and her rig—thus the mistaken illusion that a good vessel for ocean voyaging need not be able to sail well close-hauled. There will be times when, for example, a vessel must claw off a lee shore or when her destination lies a short distance to windward; however, she need not excel in this point of sailing to such a degree that she loses ability on all points of sailing. Sailing dead before the wind is sometimes necessary, so that the vessel should be capable of good (but not necessarily excellent) performance on that point of sailing. The sailing excellence one seeks in an ocean cruiser is from 3 points forward of abeam through 2 points on the quarter—or a total of 11 points. In degrees, this would be approximately from 60° to 165°, a total of 125°. In this arc is found not only the greatest speed potential but also the most comfort. Within this arc, most vessel have areas which they do not like, and by altering course by a half point—say 5°—they begin to romp right along again.

No two vessels are exactly the same—even sister ships—so it seems to me that with a little extra planning, a voyage can be enhanced by sailing that course on which the vessel performs best. *Gazelle* liked the wind from a little aft of abeam to her quarter, whereas *Apostle* liked the wind on her quarter or even a point further aft. Thus, in the trades, we planned as much as possible for a favoring wind, even if it meant sailing off course, and it always paid off. With a 36-foot waterline vessel, there is often as much as *three knots difference in speed between running and reaching!*

The difference between a direct course downwind when the vessel is sailing west and averaging, say, 110 nautical miles per day, and sailing more off the wind, averaging 156 nautical miles per day, is shown in this table:

	N. Miles Gained			N. Miles Gained	
Points	*West*	*South*	*Degrees*	*West*	*South*
1/2	45.2	15.3	5	545.4	13.6
1	43.0	30.4	10	1043.6	27.1
1 1/2	39.3	45.3	15	1540.7	40.4
2	34.1	59.7	20	2036.6	53.4
2 1/2	1/227.6	73.5	25	2531.4	65.9

Obviously, any increase in speed can justify sailing off, but time and distance must also be a factor. Over a ten-day period, one gains almost two days of sailing time—say 2 points off the direct course—provided one tacks every 24 hours. Having tacked the first time at the 12th hour, one would then cross the Rhumb line once every 24 hours at the 12th hour—for a distance sailed of 1248 N.M. by tacking, and 1100 N.M. by direct sailing, a difference of 148 miles. From the above table, it would seem the break-even point is about 1-1/2 points (or 15°) if no tacking is to be done except to return to the Rhumb line.

What about trade-wind spinnakers? I have used these sails on many of my designs and, while I have been shipmates with the rig on several vessels, I have used it on only one of my own personal vessels. It is a fine sail on some vessels, and certainly eliminates steering from dead before the wind to about two points either side of the stern. Perhaps the reason I have not used one more often is that the voyages have usually been such that the distances involved in running were too short, or that tacking was so much faster. Neither Jean nor I like long downwind runs except when the alternative is a dead beat to windward.

The trade wind spinnakers I've used were set up as Fritz Fenger first outlined, but with minor differences to suit each hull. Sometimes the seas and the vessel synchronize, and when this occurs life aboard can be miserable. I remember once when we were dipping the poles that were located 18 feet above the deck. A slight course alteration eliminated this uncomfortable motion.

My conclusion has been that the shortest distance between two points is that which is the fastest *as well as* the most comfortable.

On Vane Steering

Recently, there has been an abundance of articles and a book on self-steering and vane steering—how to build, buy, install and use them. Some of the writers are experienced ocean voyagers. Others have little or no experience at all and, like the Captain's parrot, are just along for the ride.

Unfortunately, all of the material I have read suggests that a proper ocean cruiser must have a vane or one cannot cope with a voyage except by long, tedious hours at the wheel. In their enthusiasm, the authors are quick to make the ketch, yawl and schooner obsolete because of the difficulty of fitting a vane. Then to further prove their point, the vane adherents analyze various successful applications of the vane, and contrast these achievements with what older vessels were able to accomplish without one.

Poor Joshua Slocum! He has been blamed for everything and given credit for little. According to the vane experts, he converted his sloop to a yawl to gain self-steering. I guess they never read his book, for he makes a special point of her self-steering qualities as a sloop. Moreover, he sailed *Spray* across the Atlantic to Gibraltar, then southwest to Pernambuco, where he shortened the rig—still as a sloop. It doesn't appear that he suffered the implied agonies of a sloop without a vane. Readers of his book will recall that he did break his boom, and that his decision to add the jigger was to traverse the Straits of Magellan—yet he did not add the jigger until he was at Port Angosto, the last port in the Straits of Magellan. The flying jib was not added until he was in the Pacific, at Juan Fernandez. All of this evidence shoots down their arguments.

I knew Victor Slocum and frequently discussed his father and the *Spray* with him. *Spray's* original sloop rig had almost 1000 square feet in the mainsail (about twice the area considered proper nowadays). When the rig altered, the area was reduced to about 600 square feet. I offered the opinion that the reduction for the Straits was justified since it reduced the frequency of reefing, and then, in the Pacific, more sail area was needed to achieve the satisfactory performance, so the jigger and the flying jib were added. Victor pointed out that the flying jib was not always carried, yet his father could always balance *Spray*. So another theory is shot down.

Then these "experts" have a go at the blunt hull and long keel as being the sole properties of the self-steering of *Spray*, and apply vector analysis to prove the point. Nonsense! Rubbish! What it all boils down to is, first and most importantly, that one must be a sailor to achieve such performance, for a sailor does not need theories to figure out how to sail. He just does what has to be done. Now if you give a sailor a long keel, two or more masts, short overhangs, and sail-carrying ability, as well as substantial sail area, so much the better. He will, in any case, shortly learn how his vessel wants to, and likes to sail, for his desire is to be a companion to, as well as master of his vessel.

There are instances where a vane will permit a good sailor as well as sail*er* to perform on certain courses with a finer degree of accuracy and drive. In no case, however, does this imply that common sense in the design of hulls and rigs should be abandoned to utilize such a device.

So let's face it! Vanes are usually added to many vessels because of inherent faults of the vessel itself. The faults of these vessels are based on fads of the moment. At the present time, they consist of cutaway underbodies, skeg and spade rudders, high aspect rigs, numerous headsails suited to the sloop and cutter rigs, long overhangs—all coupled with an unworkable deck loaded with winches—and a miserable interior—all at outrageous prices. It's little wonder then that the need for still another "gadget" is the solution. Vanes are also added to overcome the shortcomings of the owner who will not take the time to learn the arts of a true sailor.

Well, Joshua Slocum and Harry Pidgeon are but a two who are shaking their heads in Fiddler's Green, wondering what the world has come to. I am sure they concede that a sensible vessel for ocean voyaging may do poorly under the rating rules, and maybe not too well around the buoys, but I am also sure they must chuckle at owners expending so much time, energy and money on a gadget when, often, they could have added a mizzen mast and accomplished the same thing.

On Mr. Murphy

A leaking deck, a smoking stove, and a nagging woman are about all the burdens a man can bear, yet he probably will be plagued with more. Should he not understand the function of Murphy's Laws Relating to the Behavior of Inanimate Objects, he may be doomed to despair and frustration.

There are six general laws and, of course, dozens of variations that plague all endeavors. The best known is the first: "If anything can go wrong, it will go wrong." We tend to notice this one most often when anchoring or weighing anchor. In the first instance, the chain doesn't run out or, in the second, the anchor fouls in an apparently clear bottom.

The second law simply states that "when left to themselves, things always go from bad to worse." This applies most vividly to paint, varnish, and chafe—especially the last when it should have been eliminated in the first place and, failing that, at least should have been guarded against.

One time, aboard *Apostle*, we were maneuvering in very close quarters—so close that the spot the Harbormaster insisted we lie alongside was less than our length. With a boathouse behind us, our mizzen boom banging against pilings, and our bowsprit ready to punch a hole in the varnished transom of a huge motor cruiser ahead, the reverse gear chose that moment to lock in the "Ahead" position, and the Boden wire broke in the "Full Throttle" position! Miraculously no damage was done; however, it was a very tense 30-seconds.

This leads to the third law: "If there is a possibility of several things going wrong, the one that will go wrong is the one that will do the most damage."

On *K'ung Fu-Tse*, our new 48-foot junk, I had air-tested the fuel tanks to seven pounds pressure, which held. Later, upon filling these tanks with fuel, I found there was a "weep" from one tank—not much, mind you—perhaps two tablespoons per day at the most; but, any fuel leak, if only a drop, is too much for peace of mind. The only reasonable conclusion was that when the tank was under pressure a particle of dirt had lodged itself so as to permit a successful test, but when the fuel was put in the tank this particle became dislodged, allowing the leak. So the fourth rule applies well in this instance: "Nature always sides with the Hidden Flaw."

The fifth law is so universal that one could write a whole book about pertinent examples—to-wit: "Mother Nature is a Bitch." There have been times when I wondered if there was any kind of wind other than a headwind, or any tide other than a foul one. I remember one voyage lasting 63 days when we had: 56 days of headwinds, two gales, a hurricane, and 46 days of rain!

You have only to build one boat and make one ocean voyage to confront this next variation: "If everything seems to be going well, you have obviously overlooked something," this is the sixth law. I often get the feeling of impending doom when all is well, so I cannot say that I am really surprised when I discover that calamity has been lying just around the corner or over the horizon all the time.

It is difficult to remember all these laws or even their proper sequence, since more and more laws are being enacted every day to protect us from ourselves and to otherwise reduce the fun of sailing and freedom of personal movement as well as of the seas, so I must fall back on "Colvin's Law of Six P's": PRIOR PLANNING PREVENTS POOR PERFORMANCE—possibly!

On Misconceptions

For many years, I have been an advocate of moderately light displacement for ocean cruising, so avidly so that many readers have the notion that I would never own any other type of hull. Most of this is based on the statement I made about the modified sharpie: "Since owning *Apostle* all of my personal boats have been this type hull, nor would I return to the heavy displacement vessels after the pleasure of sailing 40-and 50-footers of the sharpie type, unless I were to move aboard permanently—as I *am* one of the pack-rat types." It is the word "unless" that is so often overlooked.

Gazelle was (and is) about the finest blue water cruiser I have either owned or sailed aboard. I often sailed her single-handed and never found her wanting in any respect. In fact, I was so satisfied that on the last voyage I was planning modifications which would alter her *once more*. We had decided to move back aboard and go cruising again, so being a good Scotsman I saw a bird in the hand as being better than one in the bush. This, of course, was not at all fair to *Gazelle*, nor to my family nor me. *Gazelle*, in conception, was a beast of pleasure and not a beast of burden. For our family use with five aboard, she was out for a few months and then home again. This does not mean that for a couple, or even a family of four, she was not a good permanent home—but for five, *and* my work, we needed more length, and for my pack-rats (they all take after me!) we needed more displacement.

My wife, Jean, was wise enough to see this and insist on a new vessel. So, sticking to my stated philosophy, I designed and built a new vessel for our living aboard needs—moderately *heavy* displacement of 25 tons, a long waterline of 41 feet (which allowed me to modify the 10-feet-of-vessel-length-per-person-to-be-accomodated rule, and thus fit five of us in 48 feet of deck length), and we still achieved shoal draft with 4'-4" draft—this time a *pure* three-masted Chinese junk. I am consistent to a point. I might add that if we were not selling the boatyard, house, and other property, and moving aboard permanently, we would still own *Gazelle* and our new vessel *K'ung Fu-Tse* would not have been designed or built.

Since there is a rule to everything, I suppose there could be a rule for selecting displacement—within my design philosophy. For straight ocean cruising with a permanent shore base, about 1-3/4 to 2-tons should be allowed for each person to be accommodated. For permanent living aboard, 4 to 6 tons per person to be accommodated seems about right. The lesser figure (4 tons) would apply to a large hull of more than 10 feet per person that must accommodate five or more persons, and the larger figure (6 tons) for a smaller vessel, say 36 feet. for two persons.

There is little justification for the heavy live-aboard vessel if one never cruises or does not intend to live aboard. The weight of her gear is such that one tends never to go sailing when just a few hours is available.

Moving Aboard

We are now living aboard *K'ung Fu-Tse*, a 48-foot Chinese junk. This is not the first time we have moved aboard, nor the first time we have lived afloat. It is, however, the first time we have completely severed ourselves from all shore ties to the extent that we have no place to which we *must* return, either through necessity or choice.

I can look back to my youth and to the many vessels in which I have served, and recall the ease of moving from one to the other by just carrying a sea bag and a sea chest. Many years later, when I had married and Jean and I had begun our family, we moved aboard *Apostle* with relative ease, to live and rear our infant daughter. Then, later, with an established shore base, it was simple to move aboard *Gazelle* for short cruises. So, there is a routine to be followed in the preparations for a life at sea.

Like everyone else, I am little more than a slave to the circumstances that surround me. One would think there would be no difference in moving aboard our new vessel; however, even though there are similarities, it is not the same. The finality of the present venture commits me to a singlemindedness regarding the sea, my family, and my vessel. I am dependent upon the vessel for shelter, transportation, comfort and survival. Happiness comes from being at sea with my family.

My world has expanded, but the space we occupy has shrunk, forcing each of us to decide which of our possessions are the most prized and will provide the needed continuity with the past. Each member has an equal area in which to stow personal possessions. There is added stowage space for our common necessities; and there is still more for *K'ung Fu-Tse* for, she, too, has requirements. The dreaded moment of truth will arrive when all available space is filled and, if more is to go in, something must go out. This final sorting out is perhaps the most difficult, for all the items are "friends" which at one time or another have brought joy, knowledge, or sorrow—and all revive memories. Our decisions must be ruthless for this is of the survival of the fittest. Nature exercises this option constantly, while ashore we are sheltered by society and its laws, which distort the natural processes, often penalizing the fittest for the continuance of the weak. Not so the sea—thus the choice of what will be taken and what must be left must always be predicated on that which allows you, an individual, to survive mentally, physically, and morally in your chosen element.

One must recognize that in such an undertaking as this there is a logical order in which all decisions must be made, and also accept that the sequence will vary for each individual, according to the circumstances of the moment. However, eventually all of the following must be considered before any degree of success can be achieved, for each is part of the whole:

1. PHYSICAL HEALTH. If less than excellent, one's limitations must be recognized and allowed for in all plans, including the vessel, her itinerary, and the certain fact that all of us are inflicted with an incurable disease—old age. In regard to the latter, however, life at sea with its continual exercise reduces the atrophying that often afflicts our bodies ashore, and adds years of usefulness to body as well as mind.

2. MENTAL HEALTH. One must be able to enjoy one's own company for prolonged periods. Voyaging, of necessity, reduces the social intercourse that many people require to exist happily. Ship's business futher reduces communal relationships other than at meals or change of watch. Furthermore, it is essential to accept other members of the crew as they are, and to trust them as well as oneself.

3. RESPONSIBILITY. For the Master, this entails a sort of alienation from the crew, and this includes man-and-wife crews. There can be only one Master on any vessel, and upon his shoulders rests, often heavily, the safety of vessel *and* crew. Sailing is not and can never be democratic; at best, it is feudal. This does not imply disagreement on destination, duration of port visits, watch standing, etc.; nor does it imply mental or physical flogging. Discipline aboard a sailing vessel must be rigidly maintained. The crew, on the other hand, must do what they are told to do without question, and must appreciate that while things might be different if they were Master, they are not; and until such time as they become Master, they must simply do as they are told.

4. SEAMANSHIP. This is all-inclusive, including sailing, navigation, meteorology, mechanics, piloting, sailmaking, and all else that it done to enable the vessel to prepare for, commence, and complete a voyage. Some of this may be learned from books; some must be learned at sea; but all must be applied with common sense.

5. THE VESSEL. There is no "ideal" vessel for ocean voyaging except at various moments in time when a vessel is—all other things considered—ideal for her intended purpose. If one is fortunate, it may remain so for many years. Each vessel has her own inherent faults and graces. The wise Master accepts these limitations and expects the vessel to do only what she is capable of doing and do it well. Except for a survival situation, the limitations on size, comfort, etc. that I have written about elsewhere still apply.

I do not feel that the length and tonnage rules that I recommend will let you down—i.e., 10 feet of vessel per person to be accommodated, and 4 to 6 tons of displacement per person (the latter tonnage figure is luxurious for living aboard). A vessel is usually more seaworthy than her crew. Conversely, a bad crew can make a vessel that is inherently seaworthy dangerous. Foremost, one factor stands out—all ocean-voyaging vessels are, to a degree, *freighters*. The more creature comforts one needs, the greater the displacement and length must be.

6. VOYAGE DURATION. Our practice has always been to prepare for one year of complete independence. At present, because we are cooking with diesel fuel on a stove that has electrically fired burners, and we have electric berth lights, our fuel consumption is about 3/4 gallon per day. Thus, after 170 days we should be looking for more fuel. However, by using alternate cooking with solid fuel (which we have), or eating less than three hot meals a day, we can remain out for a full year without foraging. By foraging (not stealing), we could remain at sea until such time as the vessel required a complete overhaul—which would be about three years.

Why Live Aboard?

The idea of living aboard, cruising, and voyaging is frequently appalling to landsmen, and beyond their comprehension. You know and I know why we are adopting—or are going to adopt—this way of life. They, on the other hand, cannot accept a simple reason or even a logical reason—only an outlandish one that *sounds* plausible to them. So, for such people, here is the reason I give.

The United States is faced with an energy crisis, and we have been asked to reduce our consumption so that, by 1980, we may "be completely independent of outside sources." After a thorough examination of my consumption, I found that to do anything less than go to sea would be unpatriotic, for I have annually consumed: 2500 gallons of gasoline in one automobile (used for both business and pleasure), 12 tires, 70 quarts of oil, 10 pounds of grease, and six quarts of anti-freeze; 1000 gallons of kerosene for heating the boat shop and general cleaning; 1100 gallons of diesel fuel to run my welding machines; 63,000 kilowatt hours of electricity; and two cords of wood for the fireplace. Cruising, I will not require goods to be delivered, and since about 150 trucks came into the yard each year, the estimated savings in truck fuel, tires, oil, etc. would be based on 15,000 road miles. I eliminate some 300 Federal, State, and local forms in triplicate or more, and their burden on the postal system. I am freeing one telephone.

There are, of course, indirect savings as well, which are difficult to estimate, but consider that I now live in shorts and a shirt and go barefoot; therefore, I annually save 10 shirts, three pairs of shoes, five pairs of trousers, innumerable pairs of socks, one jacket, 10 pairs of welding gloves, and two sweaters. Since we wear less clothing, we reduce laundry loads washed by 50 or more a year.

Furthermore, we will eat fresh foods that are locally grown, and catch fish, saving the fuel, ice, trucks, electricity, etc. required to get these items to market. We will bake our own bread, make most of our own clothes, and do our own food canning. We do not read newspapers or have a lawn to mow, all of which consume energy. Because of the foregoing, we reduce the need for more roads, improved rail systems, new airports, more governmental employees and agencies, more police, new sanitary districts, faster mail service, *ad infinitum*. Nothing short of this "plausible" explanation will suffice for the landsman. The more elaborate and fantastic, the easier it will be accepted.

Between you and me, though, the sea has always treated me kindly, perhaps because I always tried to understand and know her. My early days at sea were hard, the hours long (average about 14 hours a day), the pay and food poor but adequate; however, I learned to observe and to profit from these observations. I have been shipmates with some of the best as well as some of the worst individuals, not to mention vessels. I learned early that "all hands on deck" meant "on the double," felt the numbness of exhaustion, of "fisting" sails when my hands were stiff, cold and bleeding, of sleeping in soggy oilskins whenever there was a brief lull from another "all hands tack ship." But more vividly I remember the trades, the fair weather, sailing on a broad reach, the lee rail just awash, with all sails set and drawing. True—life has been good to me, but I have been the recipient of an abundant allotment of luck, quite often regarded by me at the time as misfortune.

If, by what I have written, said, or implied, you also decide to go to sea, I am sure you will find, as I have, that it is a good life. If you are truthful with yourself, you will find that it is not a life of Walter Mitty dreams but an exquisitely undrempt dream, alive with never-ending wonders.

It is my hope that we may someday share an anchorage; but in any case, my wish is that "Fair Winds Escort You" wherever you cruise.

Fair Winds Escort You

Good luck device used on
hou-pan-ch'uan salt junk.
Found on the stern only.